THE BIBLICAL GUIDE TO
AVOID THE PITFALLS
OF SEXUAL IMMORALITY

ADULTERY

EDWARD D. ANDREWS

ADULTERY

The Biblical Guide to Avoid the Pitfalls of Sexual Immorality

Edward D. Andrews

Christian Publishing House

Cambridge, Ohio

CHRISTIAN PUBLISHING HOUSE
CONSERVATIVE CHRISTIAN BOOKS
APOLOGETIC DEFENSE OF GOD, THE
FAITH, THE BIBLE, AND CHRISTIANITY

ADULTERY: The Biblical Guide to Avoid the Pitfalls of Sexual Immorality by Edward D. Andrews

ISBN-13: 978-1-949586-80-0

ISBN-10: 1-949586-80-4

Table of Contents

CHAPTER 1 Marriage Is a Gift From God

Ecclesiastes 4:12 Updated American Standard Version (UASV)

¹² And though a man might prevail against one who is alone, two will withstand him. A threefold cord is not quickly broken.

It would seem that no expert or anyone who has studied the situation would disagree that the institution of marriage is a dismal failure today. "Over the past several decades, the nature of marriage has changed. Many people are choosing to live their lives with partners without getting legally married, and Americans are increasingly more approving of this option. (Marquart et al., 2012). Unfortunately, people who do marry have roughly a 50 percent chance of staying married. That is equivalent to flipping a coin on your wedding day. Even for couples who stay married, many reports being unsatisfied in their relationships." Sadly, the statistics do not change just because the couple is Christian.

For those who have entered into a marriage, they might ask can they maintain and improve upon their marriage year after year. For those thinking of getting married, can they find true happiness in marriage, will it last? The answers to these questions and others are largely dependent on whether both the husband and the wife correctly understand what the Bible says to husbands and wives, fathers and mothers, and are they applying that biblical counsel in a correct and balanced manner. If we are wholeheartedly trusting in God, not depending on our own understanding, but rather seeking his will in all that we do, he will show us the path to take.' (Pro. 3:5-6) If we do those things, we will remain in God's love.

Should You Get Married?

For some, Marriage is essential for happiness, as God designed man and woman to get married. It is as though something is missing in life if one is lacking their mate. Yet, during this time while God is working out the issues that were raised by Satan in the Garden of Eden and at the beginning of the book of Job, he has encouraged some, who are able to consider remaining single, so as to serve him more fully without any distractions. Jesus spoke of singleness as being a gift. (Matt. 19:11-12) In addition, the apostle Paul spoke of the benefits of singleness. (1 Cor. 7:32-38) However, let it be known that there is no Scriptural basis for any Christian denomination or Christian leader to demand that anyone remain single. In fact, the apostle Paul warned Timothy that "in later times some will fall away from the faith, paying attention to deceitful spirits and doctrines of demons, by means of the hypocrisy of men who speak lies, ... who forbid marriage." (1 Tim. 4:1-3) There are supposed Christian denominations that have forbidden marriage among its priests for centuries. If we feel the calling to serve God more fully and want to forgo marriage during this time, make certain this is you calling and desire. If, not there is true joy and happiness within marriage if we correctly understand and apply the Bible guidance on the matter.

We do not want to cast a shadow over the institution of marriage. Marriage is also a gift from God. (Gen. 2:18) Marriage has advantages and can possibly bring many blessings. For example, the person who is in a good marriage has the best foundation for enjoying life. Children need and deserve a two-parent family that is stable, with Christian parents raising them based on Bible principles, providing love, discipline, and guidance. (Ps 127:3; Eph. 6:1-4) While raising children is the number one reason for marriage, it is not the only reason.

Ecclesiastes 4:9-12 Updated American Standard Version (UASV)

[9] Two are better than one, because they have a good reward for their labor. [10] For if they fall, one will lift up his fellow. But woe to the one who falls when there is not another[1] to lift him up. [11] Again, if two lie down together, they can keep warm, but how can one keep warm alone? [12] And though a man might prevail against one who is alone, two will withstand him. A threefold cord is not quickly broken.

The passage can be used for friendship, A Christian not separating himself from the congregation, and yes, Marriage, which is the closest friendship one, can have. The single person does not have the same assistance, comfort, and protection that married couples can share. The twofold cord can be torn but not as easy a single cord. In a marriage, the third fold of that threefold cord is God. The husband, the wife, and God make up the threefold cord. Therefore, three strands woven or braided together would be much more difficult to tear apart. When pleasing God first is the prime concern of both the husband and the wife, the marriage is then like the threefold cord. If God is truly a part of the Marriage, the union will then be very strong.

Moreover, biblically, it is only within a marriage that sexual desires can be satisfied. Within the marriage, the sexual union is biblically viewed as a source of delight or pleasure. (Pro. 5:18) When a young single person reaches the age when sexual desires are very strong, he or she may struggle with their sexual desires. If these desires are not kept under control, it could lead to unclean, sinful conduct. Paul offers us the following counsel to single people, "But if they do not have self-control, let them marry; for it is better to marry than to burn with passion."—1 Corinthians 7:9, 36; James 1:15.

Regardless of our reason to marry, we need to be realistic as well. Paul was quite realistic with those who marry "will have tribulation in their flesh." (1 Cor. 7:28) Those who marry will face difficult times and challenges that sing people do not face. Here is where we offer biblically sound information to those who choose to marry, as to how they can decrease the challenges and increase the blessings. The best way is to choose your mate wisely.

Choosing a Good Marriage Mate Based on Scripture

The Apostle Paul under inspiration gives a vital principle that we need to consider when choosing a marriage mate. "Do not be yoked together with unbelievers." (2 Cor. 6:14) What did Paul mean by 'being yoked together'? Paul was giving us an agricultural example. A yoke is a wooden frame for harnessing two draft animals to whatever they had to pull. If a donkey and an ox are yoked together, it will be two animals of a major difference in size and strength, meaning that both will suffer. That is because there will be great friction and strain because the strong animal will have to make up for the weak animal. This is the same in the marriage of a believer and an unbeliever. In a marriage between a believer and an unbeliever, there will be the same friction and strain because the believer will have to carry most of the burden being the stronger of the two. The believer will want to be faithful to God in all things and the unbeliever will likely care little about that. They will not have the same priorities in life. The believer will want to focus on Christian meetings, while the unbeliever will be focused on the desires of the flesh. Much pain and suffering will result from this. Paul thus urged Christians to marry "only in the Lord." – 1 Corinthians 7:39.

Loneliness can be a bitter storm to survive. The pain of wanting someone to love and seeing others in love can be overwhelming at times. This can move the single Christian to ignore Paul's Holy Spirit advice and decide that being unevenly yoked is better than no marriage at all, so they marry an unbeliever. It always ends up the same way, at first; it seems to have been worth it. Then, as time passes, the fleshly qualities of the unbeliever begin to take a toll. The believer begins to feel just as alone in the marriage because they cannot share the most important thing in life with their mate. Therefore, it is wise to trust God. (Ps 32:8) It is best to remain single until an opportunity come to "marry in the Lord."

Now, we must state the obvious. Not every Christian is a person worthy of marriage just because they claim to be a Christian. When choosing a mate, we need to seek out the spiritually mature. Do they regularly go to the Christian meetings? Do they prepare for those Christian meetings? Do they have spiritual goals? Do they take their walk with God serious? Do they show that they have a deep love for God? Remember, actions speak louder than words. We need to use the principles of God's Word to guide us to the mate that will compliment us. – Psalm 119:105.

Ways that You Can Prepare for a Successful Marriage

If you are considering marriage, it is best to ask yourself, "Am I truly ready?" The answer to your question does not really hinge how you feel about love, sex, companionship, or raising children. Rather, you have to think through different goals that need to consider when you are a prospective husband or wife.

If you are a young man or even an older man, consider the Proverb, "Prepare your work outside; and get it ready for yourself in the field, afterward, build your house." (Prov. 24:27) What is the meaning here? In those days, "a young Israelite who was ready to start his own family would need to build a house for his bride and get his farm operating. Which is the first priority? Proverbs advises him to do the **outdoor work first**. He should get the **fields** ready because they were his source of income. The **house** was the place that provided personal comfort, but the crops were the means for supporting the farmhouse. In short, produce before you consume. And a young person contemplating marriage should set up a means to support his family before he starts one."[2] Yes, this young man needed to consider, "Am I able to support a wife and any children that may come or are already there?" A man who fails to care for the physical, emotional, mental and spiritual needs of his family is worse than one without faith! – 1 Timothy 5:8.

Then, we turn to the woman, who must also consider what her weighty responsibilities might be. God's Word praises the skills and qualities of a wife that helps her husband, as she cares for the household. (Pro. 31:10-31) If the man and the woman rush into the marriage without considering the responsibilities that lie ahead, they are being selfish and thinking of immediate gratification. Bu rushing ahead, they are not truly considering what they need to possess in the ways of skills and qualities that add to the marriage. More importantly, they need to consider also how to prepare spiritually.

When we prepare for marriage, we need to consider the roles that God has assigned to the husband and wife. The man needs to recognize full what it means to be the head of the Christian household. This place within the marriage is not a license to act as an oppressor or some dictator. Rather, he must imitate Jesus Christ as to how he exercises headship over the congregation. Paul said, "For the husband is the head of the wife, as Christ also is the head of the congregation,[3] he himself being the Savior of the body." (Eph. 5:23) "The wife is to be subject to her husband as to the Lord.

13

This does not mean that she submits to her husband in the same way and to the same degree as she does the Lord since the husband might ask her to disobey God. Rather she serves the Lord by having a submissive heart toward her husband and by obeying him as long as it does not require her to disobey the Lord. The reason she is called upon to be subject to her husband is that the husband is the head of the wife, as Christ is the head of the church. As the church is to be subject to Christ, so the wife is to be subject to her husband. This subjection does not mean inferiority. It is clear that male and female are both created in the image of God (Gen. 1:27) and that in Christ, where personal worth is concerned, there is "neither Jew nor Greek, slave nor free, male nor female, for you are all one in Christ Jesus" (Gal. 3:28). However, in the overall scheme of things, God has placed all of us in differing positions of authority and submission. The man may be in authority at home but submissive at work. The woman may be in submission at home and in authority at work. The point is, all social order depends on people's willingness to work together and ability to determine who is the head of certain endeavors. God's intention is that the husband be the head of the relationship with his wife." [4]

If a woman has not matured enough spiritually in the faith, so she can be supportive and submissive when it comes to the authority of an imperfect husband, she should not marry. If a man has not matured enough spiritually in the faith, so he can know that he must always listen to his wife and be able to biblically decide whether her way is the best way or not and that he is not a tyrant over her, he should not marry. In other words, Scriptures have been largely misunderstood and abused by both men and women. The prospective mates must fully and accurately, know what the Bible author meant by the words that he used. Then, they need to ask themselves, "Can I accept this in my heart and apply it in my marriage?"

The marriage mates need to be prepared to care for the special needs of the other. We can apply the Apostle Paul's words to the Philippians, "Everyone should look out not only for his own interests,[5] but also for the interests of others." (Phil. 2:4) "Looking out for our own interests comes naturally. We need, and receive, no instruction for that. We are instructed to look out for **the interests of others**. We are to keep an eye out to discover ways we can help others even when they do not see they need such help. The apostle stated in Galatians 6:2: 'Carry each other's burdens, and in this way you will fulfill the law of Christ.'"[6] Paul also wrote, "let each one of you love his wife as himself, and let the wife see that she fears[7] her husband." (Eph. 5:21-33) This fear means the wife should have a deep respect, a fear of displeasing him because of her great love, not a dreadful fear or some feeling of anxiety. Max Anders writes, "In summary, she is to be subject to her husband and to respect him. **Respect** (*phobetai*) literally means "fear." It can refer, however, to the fear a person should have before God, a reverence and respect (Luke 1:50; 18:2; Acts 10:35; 1 Pet. 2:17; Rev. 14:7; 19:5). This type of reverence and regard should characterize the relationship of a wife and her husband."[8]

Therefore, the engagement, then, is not just a time for fun. It is a period where a man and a woman get to know each other. They get to learn how to deal with each other biblically. It is also a time to see if marriage is the best choice at this time, with this person. It is also a time when one needs to be very cautious and have control over themselves. While there is nothing wrong with kissing or holding your prospective marriage mate, it is dangerous to do so when alone. Being physically intimate is natural, a gift from God. However, those who love God more than their future husband or wife, will not put themselves in innocent appearing situations because to commit fornication before marriage is no way to begin a lifelong commitment to each other or God. Entering marriage after committing such a serious sin is such a terrible foundation on which you want to build. (1 Thess. 4:6) If your will cheat on God with each other because of sexual desires, does this not indicate that you may cheat on each other for those same sexual desires?

How can You Make Your Marriage Survive Your Imperfections and Human Weaknesses?

If the marriage is to survive Satan's world, your imperfection, and human weaknesses, both the husband and the wife need to have the right view of commitment. When we read romance novels or watch Hollywood movies, we always find a loving ending, which anyone would crave. However, marriage, in real life, is not a romance novel or movie. In real life, there is no end; it is an ongoing relationship, which goes on for an eternity, and was designed by God. (Gen. 2:24) It is our view of marriage that matters. A common saying is that the couple is "tying the knot." The problem with that saying is it can be viewed two different ways. First, a good knot can be tied to last as long as it is needed. Notice, as long as it is needed. What happens when you decide you no longer need the knot? Second, a knot can be untied.

The popular view of marriage today is that it is only temporary. Many couples enter marriage only thinking of their individual needs at the time. However, the moment the marriage is a challenge, they are ready to end things. NOTE: There are biblical reasons to end a marriage, such as adultery and physical, mental, emotional, and spiritual abuse. Jesus said, "What therefore God has joined together, let not man separate." (Matt 19:6) If we marry, we need to have that kind of commitment, and if it seems like a burden, marriage should not be a consideration. Again, there are reasons for leaving your marriage mate. Thus, we will offer a brief excursion here.

When you get married, the husband and the wife need to maintain the same biblical view of each other. If each one applies God's word correctly in their lives, seeing the good qualities and efforts of their spouse, the marriage will be a joy. While we are imperfect, we can still have positive views of each other. Husbands and wives need to have a positive view of their mate and make allowance for when they fall short. – Colossians 3:13.

CHAPTER 2 Surviving the First Year of Marriage

One man admitted a year into the married, "I am so surprised that my wife and I are so different!" "For example, she stays up late at night, and I like to go to bed early" He reluctantly adds, "I cannot understand her moods; they are as confusing as high school math." The thing that got him most was, "I know I was right in the disagreement we just had, but how is it that I am the one always apologizing and feeling bad." Lastly, he says, "She is so critical of how I do household chores. Nothing seems to be good enough."

The wife had some complaints of her own, "My husband barely speaks to me." She goes on, "It is just 'hello,' 'how was your day,' 'thank you,' no real meaningful conversations." She says, "Even when he asks me, how was your day, he does not really mean it because I start to tell him about my day, he moves on to what he wants to tell me." Sadly, she says, "When I am upset and want to talk about it, he starts to listen, but then he interrupts me with what I need to do to fix things. He is more into fixing problems than letting me get the problems off of my chest." She ends with how irritated she is, "Why are men so difficult to understand? How do can we make our marriage succeed?"

If you have just recently gotten married, you likely have faced similar challenges. It is weird how you never noticed these faults and shortcomings that you never noticed when you were dating or engaged. How can you lessen the impact of the "everyday troubles that married people will have"? – 1 Corinthians 7:28, Good News Translation (GNT).

First, realize this simple fact. You are newly married, and neither you nor your spouse is an expert on married life. True, maybe both of you had acquired great social skills before you met, even matured as an adult, and they may have served you well while you were dating. Let us face it; everyone puts his or her best foot forward when you are dating. Both work very hard to please the other. The skills and qualities that you and your spouse have acquired in life and throughout the dating process are like the baby steps of life. Marriage will put those skills and qualities to the test, to refine and strengthen them, if you allow that to be the case.

There are two important points here. (1) You need to ponder, consider, meditate on how you can grow and develop the skills and qualities you have. (2) Likely, life requires that you gain new one's skills and qualities. Let us just mention one in passing. From this day forward, practice thinking before you respond. Literally, when your spouse says something to you, stop, pause 3-5 seconds and think about what you are going to say. If you even think, it will hurt or harm, even in the slightest way, do not say it, let go of it. Another, your spouse does not need to know everything all the time. If there is something that happened in your day that will hurt or harm feelings in the slightest way, keep it to yourself. If a woman flirts with you in line at a restaurant and you did not reciprocate to her but instead lifted your hand and said I am happily married. There is no harm or foul here. What purpose does it serve to share that information? It is like when your wife asked you if this dress makes her look fat. You know it does and to top things of it is hideous as well. Truthfully, you can let her know that it is not good in the gentlest way possible without being frank about it.

The best way to improve your skills and qualities is to consult an expert. Once we have the advice from the expert, it is absolutely necessary that we listen to the advice. There is no greater expert than the Creator of man and women, who instituted the first marriage. (Gen. 2:22-24) Here in this book, we will quote many Scriptures. Many times, we will offer commentary on what the author meant by his words. You will notice how the Bible is able to help you overcome your weaknesses, improve the skills and qualities you have, and acquire new ones that will vastly improve your marriage. The one message that needs to be taken seriously is: apply, apply, and apply.

SKILL – Learn to communicate with each Other

Why is this such a challenge? Because you were used to thinking for one person and now you must realize that your decisions, your comments, and how you act impacts another person, namely, your spouse. When you make a decision, for example, without consulting your spouse, it makes her feel as though she is not involved in the marriage or that her voice does not matter. Worse still, at times you might talk to your friends about a decision and not even consider your spouse's input on the situation.

What is the Solution?

Keep in mind that Jesus said, "are no longer two but one flesh." (Matt. 19:3-6) In the eyes of God, no other human relationship is as important as that between a husband and a wife. If you are going to grow your relationship beyond the first year, good communication is vital.

Much of the historical narrative in the Bible is given to us so that we can learn a lesson from it. If we look at the account between God and Abraham, we see how God communicated with him. See the discussion recorded in Genesis 18:17-33. Notice how God honored Abraham. (1) God explained to Abraham what he intended to do. (2) He listened and allowed Abraham to explain his views on the situation. (3) Even God made a little adaptation based on Abraham's thoughts. You can follow this same pattern by consulting your spouse, listening to your spouse, and accommodating the spouse's concerns to the extent possible

It is best to present your thoughts to your spouse as suggestions, not final decisions or ultimatums when discussing matters that will affect your marriage. Both of you can offer your opinions and evidence that you support your spouse's insights. You need to show a gentle attitude toward everyone. – Philippians 4:5.

SKILL - Learn to be Sensitive, Thoughtful, and Perceptive

Why is this such a challenge? The world is a melting pot today, and cultures differ. Truly, even communities differ from one another. As you grew up may it was fine to offer your opinion firmly, even bluntly. There are places in Europe that an American ear would consider them to be tactless, but it is the norm there to be very direct when expressing themselves. This is something that should be overcome for the sake of the marriage.

What is the solution?

Never assume that your spouse should be spoken to or even likes to be spoken to as you have been accustom to speaking to others. (Philippians 2:3-4) What the Apostle Paul told Timothy should be applied in a marriage as well. "For a slave of the Lord does not need to fight, but needs to be kind to all, qualified to teach, showing restraint when wronged." (2 Tim. 2:24) **Tact** is the ability to avoid giving offense: skill in situations in which other people's feelings have to be considered. **Sensitive** is one who is thoughtful and sympathetic: tactful and sympathetic about the feelings of others. **Perceptiveness** in a marriage is one who is quick to understand: possessing or showing keen insight and understanding. When you find yourself upset with your spouse try to ponder how you would respond to your boss at work or your bosses' boss. Would you use the same tone, the same words, or would you choose your words wisely? True, it is sad that you would tone it down out of respect for your boss and fear of displeasing him or her, but you would not do the same for your wife out of respect and love. – Colossians 4:6.

SKILL - Learn to Grow Into Your Role within the Family

Why is this such a challenge? The husband is not used to using his headship that he never had before the marriage. This is a new role you have never had. You have normally just made your decisions without considering others. Maybe you grew up in a family where your father never consulted your mother. Thus, the friction you have been feeling at the beginning of your marriage might be because you are ruling your family like you are the king. The other side of the coin is that your new wife might be demanding of you in things like being tidier around the house. Thus, the two of you could ponder, how does it make you feel when the other is demanding?

What is the solution?

As a Christian husband, you too might be confusing what the Bible has to say about wifely subjection and what it says about the obedience of a child to his parent. (Col. 3:20; 1 Pet. 3:1) Rather, the Bible says, "a man shall leave his father and mother and be joined to his wife, and the two shall become one flesh." The wife is a compliment (or counterpart) of her husband. God never refers to the child of the house as being a complement or counterpart to the parent. Therefore, it is not honoring your wife when you treat her like a child and demand that she obey you.

Actually, the Word of God urges you to treat your wife in the same manner that Jesus Christ treats the Christian congregation. You can make it easier for your wife to respect your headship if you first respect her role within the family. You should not expect her straightaway and perfectly to express her subjection to you, she is new to her role as well. You are to love her in the same way you love and care for yourself, even in times of difficulty. (Eph. 5:25-29) If you do these things, the wife will, in turn, honor you as the husband and accept you as the God-appointed head. (1 Cor. 11:3) She will recognize that by honoring you, she is also honoring God. She will know that to reject your headship; she will be evidencing how she feels about you and God.

When you and your wife are tackling challenging issues that come up, try to focus on the challenge, not each other. You wife will love you more deeply if you give her some time to adjust to her new role. Moreover, love her more deeply if she gives you the same opportunity. Therefore, buy out the time to discuss how you are going to be patient with each other. However, the moment someone shows a little impatience, this is not the time to say, "You said you were going to be more patient with me." We all are weak, imperfect humans and are bound to fall short many times. – Ephesians 5:33.

Another thing you might try is: do not focus on the way you think you wife needs to change. Rather, you focus in on what you need to do to make changes. If she does the same thing, all will be well. You cannot change another by demanding it, but you can motive them by making your own needed changes. You might be upset by how you have fallen short ion exercising your headship, why not ask your wife where you might be able to improve. Then, apply those suggestions in your dealings with her. The wife should as you for suggestions on how she might improve as well.

If you and your wife go into marriage thinking that it is going to be nothing but bliss, you are setting yourselves up for failure from the start. You and your wife should expect to make some embarrassing mistakes as you gain experience in the marriage. While you certainly want to take your shortcomings seriously, you have to learn not to take life too seriously. You have to be able to laugh at yourself. Make it your mission to bring joy to your wife throughout the first year of marriage. (Deut. 24:5) Most of all, allow the Word of God to guide your relationship. If God is the focal point of the marriage, the relationship will grow stronger each year.

Study the Word of God together

- You and your wife should have your own personal Bible study that each of you does alone.

- You should have a family study at least two days a week. You being the head of the house, you need to prepare for the studies and make sure it runs smoothly.

- You and your wife need to prepare for all Christian meetings.

- You and your wife need to attend all Christian meetings each week, regularly.

- You and your wife need to have some evangelism program where you are sharing God's Word with others and making disciples.

CHAPTER 3 Cultivate a Lasting Love That Never Fails

Build a happy marriage. Strengthen your marriage. Develop genuine love. Cultivate a lasting love that never fails. Make your marriage grow. Cultivate romance, passion, and intimacy in your marriage.

It is the day that seems like no other, that is, the day you met the love of your life. The first few months seem like a whirlwind. You cannot get enough of each other. It is like time is standing still and you would move heaven and earth to buy out more time for each other. There are magical moments of loving expressions several times a day. There is a litany of words that convey just how deep your love runs for each other. It is as though you cannot get enough. Both of you say to each other over and over, "I do not want this to end." Both of you beg the other that the passion never ends, the romance never ends, that routine never sets in, that you never get bored with one another, or that you never want to be like other couples.

The Beginning of the End

It was inevitable and the unthinkable happens about six months in, as you look up one day and realize the relationship is not what it was. It has now become routine, there is less of everything that once was. How did this happen? Does it happen to everyone? What can be done to not allow your relationship to end up where you have grown apart? What can be done? These are important questions. They actually have balanced answers so it might be best if we offer you an answer to each before we delve into the many ways you can cultivate your love.

How did your relationship slow down from what it once was to where it has become routine? This is actually normal and to some degree perfectly fine, and even beneficial. The beginning of a relationship is very difficult on both parties because you will take time out of things you need to do, you will skip sleep to have more time, your energy and drive will be in overload. There is no way to maintain this level of passion, love, romance, and desire. However, do not let that comment lull you into thinking it is fine to let your marriage weaken to certain levels because it can fall into disrepair, boredom, lack of interest, even anger over feeling obligated to express what you once desired to express freely.

Does it happen to everyone? Yes, there is no exception to this, every couple goes through the part of the relationship where things settle into a marriage that is still filled with love and passion but realistically, not 24 hours a day.

What can be done to not allow your relationship to end up where you have grown apart? There are many ways to maintain, develop, grow, and strengthen the marriage. This takes time and effort, so if you are not up for such work, do not expect a lasting love. Now we will deal with what can be done?

Strengthen Your Marriage

Do you want to continue in your marriage where you would rather spend time with your spouse than with anyone else? A strong marriage is the result of hard work. Appreciate and value warm, intimate communication with your spouse, for it reassures them that they are loved. In this communication learn your spouse's feelings about as many things in life as possible and try to adapt your approach respectively. Try to understand each other's viewpoints. Always speak lovingly, being aware that a well-chosen word can either build up or tear down. It is the little things in a marriage that keep a marriage alive. As your marriage grows over the years, phone and text each other throughout the day just to see how the other is doing and express your love and appreciation for them.

Continue learning about each other. A strong marriage is not inactive but grows richer and stronger with time. How well do you really know your spouse? Do you understand his or her feelings and thoughts on many different matters and issues? How often do you think about your spouse? How often do you think of the wonderful qualities and characteristics that drew you to your spouse in the first place?

No human is perfect, and no marriage is perfect. And no couple is always going to agree. If you lack respect for your spouse, this will be evident in the way you communicate with each other. If this is not dealt with, the marriage could be heading for failure. The proud person will make excuses for their behavior. Rather, you should acknowledge your weaknesses as opposed to pointing at the faults of your spouse. When you are hurt, you should pursue peace, rather than be offended and then using harsh words or icy silence. Can you ever imagine life without your spouse?

Your Spouse Is Number One

Every marriage requires hard work from both the husband and the wife. If the wife is working hard to please only the husband and not herself, he will be satisfied. If the husband is working hard to please only the wife and not himself, she will be satisfied. You have to want it to make it happen. Is improving your marriage the priority? If your marriage and your spouse is important to you, they should be your primary focus of your time and efforts. Yes, of course, you take care of your children and family responsibilities too, but you never drop the effort at making your spouse number one.

Test and Examine Your Marriage

2 Corinthians 13:5 Updated American Standard Version (UASV)

[5] Keep testing yourselves to see if you are in the faith. Keep examining yourselves! Or do you not realize this about yourselves, that Jesus Christ is in you, unless indeed you fail to meet the test?

The apostle tells us that as Christians we are to test and examine whether we are maintaining and growing our faith. We can apply this same principle to our marriage. You can test and examine whether you are maintaining and growing our marriage. When was the last time that you truly took a good look at your marriage? How did you feel about what you saw? You need to buy out the time to see how each of you is doing, both in the marriage and with life in general. The goal in these tests and examinations are (1) to do it together, (2) do not talk about superficial stuff, (3) but rather discuss what is really going on in the marriage. Share insights into how you feel about each other's positives and show loving concern over things that may be troubling you. In a marriage, you must be proactive (strengthening the marriage) rather than reactive (responding to your marriage after it has entered difficulty). Like cancer to the body, you want to cut off major problems while they are small.

Realistic Expectations

Husband, your wife is not like you. Wife, your husband is not like you. When you use "should" statements, you are projecting yourself on your spouse. "You should be doing this," or "you should be doing that." Being one with your spouse does not mean 100% agreement on every detail of life. Think about the best of your spouse. Now, understand he or she is not perfect. Moreover, if you fall into comparing your spouse with the ideal perfect spouse in your mind, then he or she is doomed to failure and you will believe that you are in a bad marriage. Neither of you is the enemy of a happy marriage that prize belongs to Satan, who does not want you to have a happy marriage.

Cultivate Intimacy

Do not take everything too serious. Be able to joke with each other without there being repercussions if a joke falls flat or ends up being insensitive. Be imaginative and be willing to have fun even during the hard times.

Share your life with each other. Find something in life that you both can enjoy together. Doing things together will keep the friendship part of your relationship strong.

Keep the flame alive. All too often the relationship can grow routine, boring and tiring without our ever noticing. You go from not being able to get enough of each other to feel as though you are obligated to show affection. When things have calmed after the storm of love at the beginning, realize that you do have obligations outside of your spouse in life. However, this does not mean that you cannot show expressions of love throughout every day. Paul told the Ephesians that you should never go to bed angry. You should never go through your day without having made several brief expressions of love to your spouse and reciprocating the ones that he or she has shown you.

You need to be physical with your spouse every day. You need to kiss, to touch, to hold and hug, to hold hands, and yes make love. When you and your spouse are physical with each other, you stay in a place of trust and love with each other.

Put your love into words every day. You need to affirm your love in words to your spouse every day. You can text, you can call, you can visit, and offer genuine expressions of love. This will encourage a very personal connection with your spouse. This will cultivate intimacy as you open your heart up to your spouse.

Do intimate things together often with your spouse. You can go walking together. You can watch a sunrise or a sunset. You can walk through a park. You can go out to romantic restaurants. You can spend a weekend away at a romantic place. You can go to the movie theater. Whether you know it or not, intimacy is being prepared to share the good, the bad, and the ugly. Be sure to talk to your spouse about how he or she impacts your heart.

Communicate on major and important issues. You can talk about future goals, parenting, finances, politics, and religion. This ability to talk about the deeper things in life can be difficult at first but it is like anything if you do not give up, over time it will become easier. You must be willing to join in meaningful conversation so that you two can get to know each other better.

CHAPTER 4 Making Christian Marriage a Success

Ephesians 5:33 Updated American Standard Version (UASV)

[33] However, let each one of you **love his wife as himself,** and let the wife see that **she fears[1] her husband.**

For the wife, this fear is to have such awe or respect for a person as to involve a measure of fear, to fear, to show great reverence for, to show great respect for the husband. The joy for the groom on the wedding day when he sees his beautiful wife coming down the aisle is limitless. Almost all dating experiences that end in marriage have a similar beginning, in that, the couple's love for each other grew so much that it led to the point of wanting to marry. The vows were that they would remain faithful to each other forever in both good times and bad times. What some are unaware of is, after the wedding, both the husband and the wife will have to make changes if the marriage is to be a success. Our Creator wants us to be happy and enjoy life together as married couples. It will be successful only if it is grounded in his Word. (Pro. 18:22) Even with God's Word, we are still imperfect humans and we will have "will have tribulation in the flesh." (1 Cor. 7:28) How can married couples lessen those problems? In addition, how can we make Christian marriage a success?

One of the leading qualities in the Bible is love. The thing is, there are different kinds of love that go into a marriage. For instance, the husband and the wife must show tender affection as well as romantic love. The apostle Paul tells the husband that he is to **"love his wife as himself."** "This is Paul's third command for the husband to love. While society pressures a man to assert his manhood by snubbing his wife and her wishes, the mature Christian husband does not have to prove anything to anybody. He is free to weigh the needs and wishes of each family member and make decisions in their best interests."[2] It is love based on the principle that creates a marriage, which is truly successful.

Responsibilities of Marriage the Husband and the Wife

---

[1] to have such awe or respect for a person as to involve a measure of fear—'to fear, to show great reverence for, to show great respect for.'

[2] Kenneth L. Boles, *Galatians & Ephesians*, The College Press NIV Commentary (Joplin, MO: College Press, 1993), Eph 5:33.

The apostle Paul wrote, "Husbands, love your wives, just as Christ also loved the congregation and gave himself up for her." (Eph. 5:25) Husbands, would you die for your wives? "After instructing wives to be subject to their husbands, he instructs husbands to love their wives so completely and so righteously that the wife need never fear or suffer from her life of submission. Husbands are to **love [their] wives just as Christ loved the church**. How did Christ love the church? He **gave himself up for her**. Jesus dedicated his life to the establishment and welfare of the church. He ultimately gave his life for the church. To that degree, and of that quality, the husband is to love his wife. He is to give himself up for her. He is to dedicate his life to the physical, emotional, and spiritual welfare of his wife. Following the example of Christ, he is to give his wife not only all that he has but also all that he is. When a husband loves his wife so completely, the wife need never fear submission."[3] (See John 13:34, 35; 15:12-13)

The husband and the wife vowed to love each other through the good and the bad times. What kind of love can help a husband and wife in difficult times? Paul wrote that love "bears all things, believes all things, hopes all things, [and] endures all things. Love never fails." (1 Cor. 13:7-8) "**Love ... always protects.** Major English Bible versions translate the term *protects* (*stego*) very differently from one another. The word can mean "to endure" or "to cover, protect." If Paul had in mind the concept of endurance, he meant that love bears with many offenses and does not stop loving even under the strain of difficulties imposed by others, even going so far as to love enemies (Luke 6:27). If he had in mind the concept of covering, then he may have meant that love will not seek to expose the sins of others. Love handles the sins of others in ways that will not bring exposure or shame. It is evident that Paul limited such endurance or protection. For example, he instructed Timothy that "those who sin are to be rebuked publicly" (1 Tim. 5:20). Likewise, he called public attention to the strife between Euodia and Syntyche (Phil. 4:2). He commanded the Corinthians to stop tolerating the man who had his father's wife (1 Cor. 5:1–13). Wisdom is required to know when and how to protect or to expose, and love always tends to protect. **Love ... always trusts.** Perhaps this characteristic of love is best expressed in contemporary English idiom as: "Love gives the benefit of the doubt." Suspicion and doubt toward others do not indicate affection or love. On the contrary, when someone loves with Christlike love, he entrusts himself to the person he loves time and again. Still, love does not demand that a person trust even when the basis for trust has been destroyed. Love does not give the "benefit" when there is no "doubt." In these circumstances trust is folly. Yet, the general

---

[3] Max Anders, *Galatians-Colossians*, vol. 8, Holman New Testament Commentary (Nashville, TN: Broadman & Holman Publishers, 1999), 174.

practice of those who love is to trust the good intentions of others as much as possible. **Love ... always hopes.** Loving someone requires maintaining a measure of optimism on that person's behalf. Hope is an attitude that good will eventually come to those who may now be failing. Failure invades every Christian's life, and it often causes others to give up on the one who fails. Yet, Christians who love continue to hope for the best. This optimism encourages others to keep moving forward. This hope is based not on the Christian, but on Christ. The hope of each Christian is that Christ will preserve him to glory. When a brother falls, it is Christ who picks him up and makes him stand (Rom. 14:4). Christ is the one who promised to finish the work he began. Optimism can also become foolishness and wishful thinking. For example, Paul did not believe that the incestuous man at Corinth would repent without undergoing church discipline. **Love ... always perseveres.** Loving someone is easy when the other person does not challenge one's affections by offending or failing. Love's quality becomes evident when it must endure trials. The New Testament encourages Christians to persevere in their Christian walks (1 John 5:2–5). Here Paul had in mind particularly the need to persevere in love for others. Christians should look to the length and perseverance of Christ's love as the standard for their own."[4]

The husband is to be the head of the house, how does he care for this responsibility? Paul wrote, "Wives, be in subjection to your own husbands, as to the Lord. For the husband is the head of the wife ..." (Eph. 5:22-23) What did Paul mean? "While submission 'to one another' introduces this command, it would be a distortion of what Paul said if one were to teach that husbands should submit to their wives just as wives submit to their husbands. There is a general sense, of course, in which a husband must put the wellbeing of his wife or children ahead of his own happiness—this will be thoroughly addressed in vv. 25–33. But this does not eliminate the more specific roles in which wives are to submit to husbands, children to parents, and slaves to masters.[5] Having said this, let us qualify the wife's submissive role. (1) It is a position the wife willingly chooses to assume; the husband is nowhere authorized to put his wife in subjection. (2) It is a duty the wife owes because her Lord deserves it, even if her husband does not. (3) It is a limited submission, paralleling the limited submission Christians give to the delegated authority of government (Rom 13:1–2; Acts 4:19–20; 5:29). (4) The word 'obey,' suitable for children (6:1) and slaves (6:5) is not used of wives. **[as to the Lord.]** Christian wives are submissive to their husbands as

[4] Richard L. Pratt Jr, *I & II Corinthians*, vol. 7, Holman New Testament Commentary (Nashville, TN: Broadman & Holman Publishers, 2000), 232–233.

[5] Andrew T. Lincoln, *Word Biblical Commentary, Volume 42: Ephesians* (Thomas Nelson, 1990), p. 366. It should also be noted that the parallel in Col 3:18ff. does not mention mutual submission; it begins with a straightforward imperative command.[5]

one aspect of their obedience to Christ. This implies that the wives' ultimate reward comes from the Lord, whether they are adequately appreciated by their husbands or not. **[For the husband is the head of the wife]** The specific basis of the submission of the wife is that God has set the husband in the family as its "head" (κεφαλή, *kephalē*). Some have argued that this word means only "source,"[6] but the lexical evidence[7] and Paul's own usage in 1:22 are conclusive in support of the meaning "leader" or "ruling authority." In Eph. 1:22 Paul says that God "subjected" (ὑποτάσσω, *hypotassō*) all things under Christ's feet and that Christ was appointed to be "head" (*kephalē*) over all things. Now, in the context of chapter five, Paul clearly intends to use these keywords in the same sense."[8] "In this context the word 'head' has the idea of authority attached to it after the analogy of Christ's headship over the church."[9]

A marriage will be strong if Paul's advice to the Colossians is followed. Both the husband and the wife need to be "putting up with one another and forgiving one another. If anyone should have a complaint against another, forgiving each other; as the Lord has forgiven you, so you also must forgive." (Col. 3:13-14) What did Paul mean? "The idea of putting up with the abuses and offenses of others continues with Paul's call to **bear with each other**. Believers are to go beyond quiet resignation positively to **forgive whatever grievances [they] may have against one another**. Believers have been fully forgiven by Christ (2:13–14), and the forgiven are obligated to become forgivers. The standard for this forgiveness is Christ himself. Paul saves the most important item of clothing for last. Without love, all the other virtues may amount to mere moralism and little else (a thought found also in 1 Cor. 13:1–3). When love is present, there is harmony and unity in the community. It is not clear whether **love** binds the virtues together, completing a lovely garment of Christlike character, or whether **love** binds

---

[6] See S. Bedale, "The Meaning of *kephalē* in the Pauline Epistles," *JTS* n.s. 5 (1954) 211–215. More recently, see George Howard, "The Head/Body Metaphors of Ephesians," *NTS* 20 (1974) 350–356; and Berkeley and Alvery Mickelsen, "The 'Head' of the Epistles," *CT* 20 (1981) 264–267.

[7] Wayne Grudem in an exhaustive survey of Greek literature could not find a single instance where *kephalē* has the clear meaning of "source." See his "Does KEPHALE Mean 'Source' or 'Authority Over' in Greek Literature? A Survey of 2,336 Examples," *TrinJ* 6 NS (1985) 38–59. The uses of *kephalē* in ancient literature are consistent with this dictum of Aristotle: "The rule of the household is a monarchy, for every house is under one head" (*Pol.* 1255b).

[8] Kenneth L. Boles, *Galatians & Ephesians*, The College Press NIV Commentary (Joplin, MO: College Press, 1993), Eph 5:22–23.

[9] F. F. Bruce, The New International Commentary on the New Testament: The Epistles to the Colossians, to Philemon and to the Ephesians (Eerdmans, 1984), p. 384.

the members of the community together in mature oneness. Perhaps the ambiguity is intentional. Both ideas make good sense."[10]

Imperfection means that both the husband and the wife will make mistakes. This love is shown in that they marriage mates do "not keep a record of wrong." (1 Cor. 13:4-5) Disagreements are bound to happen more than we might like to admit because the husband and wife were raised in different social settings, different teachers, different friends, different parents, and so on. When these arise, it is best to follow Paul's counsel. "Be angry, and yet do not sin;[11] **do not let the sun go down on your anger,** [27] nor give place[12] to the devil." (Eph. 4:26-27) Both should be eager to say, "I am deeply sorry for hurting you."

Tenderness in Your Marriage

What guidance does the Bible give us regarding sexual relations in marriage? Why do marriage mates need to show tenderness? The Creator offers marriage mates great advice, so as to have a proper understanding of sex in their marriage. (See 1 Cor. 7:3-5.) Both the husband and the wife need to consider the feelings and needs of each others. If a husband is not tender, loving and affectionate with his wife, she may not truly enjoy their sexual relationship. He might fill her physical need to a degree but not her emotional needs. The apostle Peter wrote, "Husbands, live with your wives in an understanding way …" (1 Pet. 3:7) In other words, sexual relations in a marriage should never be forced, demanded or coerced. It should never be used as a tool for punishing one's spouse. Rather sexual relations should come naturally. The moments of sex within the marriage should be the right time for both the husband and the wife.

How are we to understand Peter's words that "husbands, [should] live with your wives in an understanding way"? "Husbands should be **considerate** as they relate to their wives. This word (*gnosin*) carries the meaning of "wisdom and understanding." Husbands should approach their marriage relationship intelligently. They are to live with their wives according to knowledge, not fantasy. Marriage is a real-life relationship, not a soap-opera drama. To live with your wife and demonstrate wisdom suggests a deep desire to understand your wife, to get to know her at more than just a surface level. It suggests a sensitivity to her needs and a desire to respond to these needs knowledgeably. In many ways, this sounds like

---

[10] Max Anders, *Galatians-Colossians*, vol. 8, Holman New Testament Commentary (Nashville, TN: Broadman & Holman Publishers, 1999), 331.

[11] A reference to Ps 4:4

[12] Or *an opportunity* to the devil

submission, although the language is different. It hints at the concept of mutual submission (see Eph. 5:21). Beyond this, husbands are to **treat** their wives **with respect.** "Treat" has a special significance. Classical Greek writers always used it in reference to what is due from one person to another. The giving of respect or honor to your wife is not simply a "nice guy" kind of thing to do. It is the husband's recognition of her because it is her due. This emphasis is reiterated in the word *respect.* This word is sometimes translated as 'price' or 'precious.' It indicates value and esteem. It suggests the giving of respect because a wife is precious to her husband."[13]

Song of Solomon 1:2; 2:6 Updated American Standard Version (UASV)

[2] May he kiss me with the kisses of his mouth!
For your love is better than wine;

[6] His left hand is under my head,
    and his right hand embraces me!

Husbands and wives should be tender with each other in sexual relations. Both need to consider the needs of the other first. If the husband is tenderly and passionately try to fill the needs of the wife before himself and the wife is tenderly and passionately try to fill the needs of the husband, it will be the best experience. "1:1 Marriage is the context in which physical passion and pleasure is set free. The kiss is a universal expression of desire and affection, and the woman (she is called Shulammite in 6:13) expresses her desire for her lover to kiss her and to kiss her deeply and repeatedly. The senses of touch and taste both came together, and the resulting passion was more than she could handle. She said, Your love is more delightful than wine. By describing his romantic, affectionate kisses in this way, she was saying; I find the touch of your lips and the embrace of your mouth sweet, powerful, intoxicating. It sweeps me off my feet. It sets my head spinning. The passionate kiss, we have discovered, is a sign of a healthy, romantic marriage, even more than sex. "The passionate kiss (average length one minute) reveals a lot about your relationship. Considered even more intimate than sex, passionate smooching is one of the first things to go when spouses aren't getting along" (Marriage Partnership, 10). 2:6 In the passion of their love, Shulammite had not lost sight or sense of the warmth, intimacy, and security of their relationship. With one hand he cradled her head. With the other he held and caressed her. It is interesting that the word embrace is used in the Old Testament "both of a friendly greeting (Gen. 48:10) and of sexual union (Prov. 5:20)" (Carr, 93). He was her friend and

---

[13] David Walls and Max Anders, *I & II Peter, I, II & III John, Jude*, vol. 11, Holman New Testament Commentary (Nashville, TN: Broadman & Holman Publishers, 1999), 50.

her lover. Both were important to her. Both are important to all women. No man should forget this."[14]

When our love for God is greater than the love of self, we will not allow anyone to threaten our marriage. Some have allowed their eye to wonder in looking at things they ought not. Jesus said, "Everyone who looks at a woman with lust for her has already committed adultery with her in his heart." (Matt. 5:27-28) The Greek behind "lust," ἐπιθυμία [epithumia] is a strong desire to have what belongs to another, as well as becoming involved in anything that is morally wrong, i.e., coveting, lusting, evil desires, and the like. We need to continue to develop and grow our love for both God and our spouse. We would never dream of cheating on God, nor should we ever look at another woman with lust or passion. We must keep in mind God knows every thought we have, even if our wife does not. Moreover, we have to live with our own internal guilt and shame as we hid secret sexual lusting. We need to strengthen our desire to be loyal to both God and our marriage mate.

Problem In the Marriage

Marriage will not be the fantasy that we may have had when growing up. Marriage involves two grown adults dealing with each other's weaknesses and raising children in the Christian faith while trying to cope with Satan's world. These problems within marriage have caused the divorce rate among Christians to be just as high as the unbelievers. Again, the Bible makes allowances for a divorce in the case of adultery and even if a mate is abusive and will not reconcile and repent. God never intended anyone of his servants to live a life with an abusive spouse. For more on this see What is the Scriptural Basis for Divorce and Remarriage Among Christians?[15] What are some reason for separation and possibly divorce? You, the husband willfully refuses to support your family financially, so much so, that they go without money and food. The spouse is abusing the other physically, mentally, and emotionally without any true repentance.[16]

---

[14] Moore, David; Anders, Max; Akin, Daniel. Holman Old Testament Commentary Volume 14 - Ecclesiastes, Song of Songs (p. 145, 184). B&H Publishing. Kindle Edition.

[15] https://christianpublishinghouse.co/2016/10/05/what-is-the-scriptural-basis-for-divorce-and-remarriage-among-christians/

[16] **Repentance:** The (Gr. *metanoeo* and *metamelomai*) means to repent, to change one's way, repentance. It means that we change our mind as to our sinful action or conduct, being dissatisfied with that personality trait. We feel regret, contrition, or compunction, for what we have done or failed to do. We change our way of life because we have changed our view, our way of thinking, our mindset, our attitude, our disposition with regard to out sinful behavior. We have a change of heart and mind, abandoning our former way of thinking, feeling and acting. The result is our becoming a new self, with new behavior, and having a genuine regret over our former ways. No one can testify but our own spirit that we have repented; we may make professions of repentance, and the world may believe we are

Another biblical ground for separation and possible divorce is when one spouse makes it impossible for the other to serve God, endangering his or her spiritual life.

It is the biggest shocker and test of marriage when a Christian couple comes to realize that marriage is not what they had dreamed it would be and they now are very disappointed, even angry. They had this blissful picture of some romantic comedy television show, or some Nicholas Spark novel. Do not get me wrong, it can be those things, but it is not always, every day those kinds of things. There is much work, pain, and even heartache in all marriages. **In the movies,** the couple wakes up in bed together, looking just as good as when they went to bed. They roll over and passionately kiss each other, which leads to this heavenly sexual experience. **In real life,** the next morning after the first honeymoon night, the couple wakes up next to bad breath, disheveled hair, and nothing like in the movies. Welcome to marriage. Often, the problems initially arise because the couples were brought up in two different settings and they react emotionally different from one another. He sees the in-laws in one like, she sees the money completely different (some stereotyping here), they disagree on how to raise the children or even if they are to have children. The good news is they have the good news of God's Word to guide them.

The Priority In Your Marriage

Our priority in marriage is our love of God followed by our love for our spouse. While we do not neglect our spouses for the love of God, both husband and wife need to give the worship of God priority. (Matt. 6:33) We need to accept the guidance found in the inspired, fully inerrant, authoritative Word of God. (Ps. 119:105) This means that we need to make Christian meeting attendance a priority. (Heb. 10:24-25) We need to have a personal study of God's Word. (Ps. 119:97) The husband and wife also need to study God's Word together. (Eph. 5:25-26) Both need to prepare for Christian meetings, where they know what is being studied that day. (Heb. 5:11-14) Moreover, as a family and individually, we need to share God's Word with others. – Matthew 24:14; 28:19-20; Ac 1:8.

---

thoroughly sincere, but our own spirit may tell us that our profession is false. In other words, genuine repentance will bring about results that we know to be true.–Matt. 3:2; 12:41; Mark 1:15; Lu 10:13; 15:10; 17:3; Ac 2:38; 3:19; 17:30; 2 Cor. 12:21; Rev. 2:5-3:19.

CHAPTER 5 Why Pausing Before You Speak Does Not Really Work

In an online article titled 18 Ways to Keep Your Relationship Strong, it reads, "**Keep the playfulness alive.** We all love to play, regardless of our age. Do the following: have fun together; do something ridiculous together, and just let go. In addition, the next time that your partner says something that bothers you, try responding with a joke instead of getting defensive."[17] One loving woman responded to this by saying, "It is difficult to respond with a joke when something our partner said annoyed us."

Another online article says, "Here's an amazingly simple thing you can do in your daily life that can work serious wonders. Just take a slight pause before you speak."[18] This is a common thought by persons trying to help us improve our friendships as well as our relationships. However, I would say they **have only touched on half** of the answer. Without that other half of the answer, the pause really does not help. Before we offer the other half of the answer, let's take a pause to explain the obstacles that stand in our way.

There are four factors that contribute to our getting upset or angry at what someone says to us. **(1)** We are imperfect and live in an imperfect world, compounded by the fact that God's Word says we are **mentally bent and lean toward doing bad.** We read, "When the LORD saw that the wickedness of man on the earth was great and that the whole bent of his thinking was never anything but evil, the LORD regretted that he had ever made man on the earth." (Gen. 6:5, AT) **(2)** We have a wicked spirit creature, Satan the Devil, who is misleading the entire world of humankind. We read, "Be sober-minded; be watchful. Your adversary the devil prowls around like a roaring lion, seeking someone to devour." (1 Pet 5:8, ESV) **(3)** We live in a world that caters to the imperfect flesh. We read, "For all that is in the world—the desires of the flesh and the desires of the eyes and pride in possessions, is not from the Father but is from the world. And the world is passing away along with its desires, but whoever does the will of God abides forever." (1 John 2:16-17) **(4)** We are unable to understand our inner person, which the Bible informs us is wicked: "The heart is deceitful above all things and desperately sick; who can understand it?" The apostle Paul tells us, "just as sin came into the world through one man, and

---

[17] 18 Ways to Keep Your Relationship Strong (Saturday, September 16, 2017) https://daringtolivefully.com/keep-your-relationship-strong
[18] Tool: Pause Before You Speak (Saturday, September 16, 2017) http://acleanmind.org/tools-techniques/tool-pause-before-you-speak/

death through sin, and so death spread to all men because all sinned." There is only one major factor in all four parts that will have an effect on the other two, **you**. Jeremiah 17:9; Romans 5:12.

Yes, we create our own stress when someone says something that we feel is unloving or unkind. Because **(1)** we do not understand our true imperfection, and our imperfection is easily misled by point number **(2)**, Satan. Moreover, we are easily enticed by point number **(3-4)**, the world and its desires, as well as our heart. We read, "But each person is tempted when he is lured and enticed by his own desire. Then desire, when it has conceived gives birth to sin, and sin, when it is fully grown, brings forth death." (Jam 1:14-15, ESV) Only by an active faith in Christ, and a true understanding of our imperfection, can we hope to function in an imperfect world, defeat Satan, gain control over our imperfect flesh, allow God to read our heart and help us **not** to fall victim to our own desires of the eyes. Now, let us get to that second half of our Pause before you speak.

The Bible tells us that **(1)** we are mentally bent toward evil, **(2)** we have an inner heart that is treacherous and we cannot fully understand it. This means that no human can go without ever saying something hurtful, unloving, or unkind to the people they love. It is impossible. If one of the mates has the mindset that they "should" be able to, there is no way for that person to grow in the relationship until he or she recognizes our imperfection as true. The above also has an impact on what we do when we paused before we respond.

If we just pause before we speak, our mind that is bent toward evil and our treacherous heart will feed us inappropriate thoughts, which will only upset us more. What can we do? We must pause **and reason with ourselves** during that pause. First, we need to identify when a comment to us is upsetting. We will feel a tenseness in our chest. We will feel our blood pressure rise. We will feel our heartbeat quicken. We will feel tense all over. Our mentally bent mind will begin to race with thoughts. If we feel these things, it is paramount that we **pause and ponder**. That is the second half of the answer, *ponder*. We are going to use a couple as our example. The husband has an irrational thought and before he can stop himself, he says something offensive to his wife. She immediately has the above physical, mental and emotional reaction.

Pause and Ponder

She will pause and say the following things to herself:

- What was his intent when he said that? Did he willfully mean to cause me harm? Or, is it his mentally bent imperfect mind and treacherous heart speaking?

35

- I know that he truly loves me very much. So, it is likely not intentional. He just misspoke.

- Every day, he expresses his love and concern. This comment is not what that loving man would say if he thought it through.

The most important equation in this **pause and ponder** is the word *intent*. The second most important equation is the person's *character*. Intent means that the mate willfully and intentionally, purposely meant to hurt his or her mate. If you deduce that the person had no intention of hurting you, it will ease your tension. Now, what is the mate's character? If the mate 95 percent of the time says loving, caring, thoughtful comments to you; then, this means his hurtful comment is out of character, not really him. If it is the mate's sinful nature, human weakness, his or her imperfection that brought about the hurtful comment, Jesus said we are to forgive him or her an unlimited number of times. We go to God every day with our sins and are very grateful that God is so gracious, so as to forgive us because we are repentant and sorry for our human weaknesses. Therefore, we should be quick to forgive others for their transgressions against us.

NOTE: This unlimited forgiving does not apply to emotional, mental, or physical spousal abuse. In this case, separation is best until the offender seeks and receives help. If the offender is unwilling to acknowledge, accept his or her abuse, as well as refusing any kind of mental health treatment; then, separation may very well become divorce.[19]

---

[19] https://christianpublishinghouse.co/2016/10/05/what-is-the-scriptural-basis-for-divorce-and-remarriage-among-christians/

CHAPTER 6 Strengthen Your Marriage Through Good Communication

A husband should love his wife so much that he would rather spend time with her than anyone else. She should make the husband happier each day, and her love should comfort us in difficult times. As the years pass in your marriage, never let difficult times cause you to go without communicating your love. Good communication will grow the trust between you and your wife, making the bond even stronger. Good communication will draw the two of you closer to God each day as well.

This first paragraph is a realistic expectation. Even though there will be communication problems at times. You and your wife are different in so many ways and imperfect. (Rom. 3:23) The two of you came from different cultures even if you were raised in the same country. There are some, who get married to someone from another country, who even speaks a different language. Therefore, you undoubtedly will have different ways of communicating. If you are going to communicate well, it will take much work on the part of the both of you.

Yes, all strong marriages that last forever take hard work, but it will bring great joy and pleasure to you and your wife. (Eccl. 9:9) Consider the love of Isaac and Rebekah from the Bible. (Gen. 24:67) The Scriptures show that they kept the love alive in their marriage for many decades. We see couples on news channels today being celebrated because they have been married for 70-80 years. How have they been able to accomplish this? They have grown or matured as a couple to the point where they can talk about their thoughts and feelings in an honest but kind way. They have developed the biblical qualities of understanding, love, respect, and humility.

Showing Understanding

Proverbs 16:20 Updated American Standard Version (UASV)

20 The one **who understands** a matter finds success,
   and blessed is he who trusts in Jehovah.

Max Anders writes, "Trusting God translates into attentiveness to his words. The two parts of this verse make clear that the person who trusts in the LORD is the one who ponders or takes note of the word of instruction which God gives."[20] Think this through; so that you have understanding,

---

[20] Anders, Max. Holman Old Testament Commentary - Proverbs (p. 96). B&H Publishing. Kindle Edition.

the differences between a man and a woman are on purpose by the Creator. Men, do not be angered that your wife is so different. God made man and woman complement each other. This means that man and women were made different so they could complete each other. This explains why women communicate differently than men. It is true; most women love to talk about how they feel, their friends and family, the different personal things of life. Men, having a loving and honest communication will help your wife to feel loved. It is also true that many men do not like talking about their feelings, and would rather talk about activities, problems, and solutions. Men also desire respect. Remember, these are inborn characteristics, God-given.

If you are going to communicate well, it will take much work on the part of the both of you. Understanding is the only thing that will shine a light on how these differences actually help the husband and wife to complement each other. You and your wife are mentally wired differently on purpose, so as to balance each other as counterparts. However, you being the analytical man that you are, you are likely thinking, "if we are made different on purpose, why must I learn to listen and even talk about my feelings if God made us this way?" Yes, this is very insightful on your part, which is what gets you into trouble with your wife. God made man and woman perfect, with their characteristics and qualities balanced just right. However, once sin came into the world (Gen. 3:1-6, Rom. 3:23; 5:12) so that both man and woman are missing the mark of perfection and these characteristics and qualities became out of balance. It is by Holy Spirit, the mind of Christ, and a biblical mindset that the husband and wife have, which can get them back into balance.

In many cases, you are ready to offer solutions to the problem the moment you hear it rather than listen to your wife, who wants to be heard. This is very frustrating to your wife because you will cut her off and offer your superficial advice on what the two of you should do. You are looking for a solution; she is trying to express her feelings. You are simply looking for a quick solution to the problem. You have likely learned by now that your wife only wants you to listen to her.

Proverbs 18:13 Updated American Standard Version (UASV)

[13] If one gives an answer before he hears,
  it is his folly and shame.

On this verse, Max Anders writes, "Jumping to conclusions is a special temptation for the self-important. They announce the solution before they have fully heard the problem. This is often a symptom of people who are arrogant, unteachable, or prejudiced. They have no interest in hearing the facts or anything else that might contradict their opinions."[21] Once you understand your wife's feelings, you will treat her in such a way that she feels loved. You must listen, really listen, so she knows that her feeling are important to you. (1 Pet. 3:7) Your wife, in turn, will do her very best to understand better how you think. When you and your wife follow Bible principles, you will make wise decisions together, leading to a long happy marriage.

Wise King Solomon writes, "There is an appointed time for everything ... a time to be silent and a time to speak." (Eccl. 3:1, 7) In time, your wife will learn the best times to bring certain things up and other times not to mention certain things at all. For example, you might be overwhelmed with work, stressed about things, so she holds off telling you something until a better time. Solomon also wrote, "Like apples of gold in silver settings is a word spoken at the right time." (Prov. 25:11) On this, Anders writes, "An appropriate, well-timed saying can be as attractive and valuable as a fine piece of metalwork, apples of gold in settings of silver. Note that the apples are enhanced by the fine setting, just as the saying is "apt" precisely because it comes in the right context, carefully timed for the situation."[22]

It is not enough that you learn to listen attentively to your wife; you must also learn to talk about your own feelings. You, in time, will learn to tell your wife what is deep inside your heart. In time, you will find that while you are still a little uncomfortable talking about your problems, doing so will make you feel better, as you are getting it off your chest and sharing the burden with the one who loves and supports you most, your wife. You need to go to God in prayer, asking for the right words when talking with your wife.

Being that you and your wife are different and inherited sin has misaligned your good characteristics and qualities, you will have to work hard to change the way you communicate. You need to grow the desire to be more effective in your communication skills. The irony is man will spend hundreds if not thousands of hours becoming a more effective communicator in his witnessing to strangers, as a part of his ministry. Yet, he can be slow to do the same thing to the most important person in his life. As long as God is central, things will get better in the communication. – Psalm 127:1.

---

[21] Anders, Max. Holman Old Testament Commentary - Proverbs (p. 211). B&H Publishing. Kindle Edition.

[22] Anders, Max. Holman Old Testament Commentary - Proverbs (p. 210). B&H Publishing. Kindle Edition.

Growing Your Love for One Another

Love is the most important quality in a marriage. Paul said, "above all these things put on love, which is a perfect bond of union." (Col. 3:14) "Without love, all the other virtues may amount to mere moralism and little else (a thought found also in 1 Cor. 13:1–3). When love is present, there is harmony and unity in the community. It is not clear whether **love** binds the virtues together, completing a lovely garment of Christlike character, or whether **love** binds the members of the community together in mature oneness. Perhaps the ambiguity is intentional. Both ideas make good sense."[23] Love also binds the husband and wife together in mature oneness.

You and your wife need to continue to make an effort to learn more about each other. "Looking out for our own interests comes naturally. We need, and receive, no instruction for that. We are instructed to look out for **the interests of others**. We are to keep an eye out to discover ways we can help others even when they do not see they need such help. The apostle stated in Galatians 6:2: "Carry each other's burdens, and in this way you will fulfill the law of Christ."[24] Yes, we especially need to look out for the interests of our spouse.

Growing Your Respect for One Another

This book is about making your marriage the best that it can be by way of God's Word. However, we are also dealing with realistic expectations. Even the happiest marriage is not perfect. If you speak harshly to your wife, you are not **showing her the respect** that she deserves. If there is no respect, the marriage is doomed.

James 3:7-10, 17-18 Updated American Standard Version (UASV)

[7] For every kind[25] of beast and bird, of reptile and sea creature, can be tamed and has been tamed by mankind. [8] But no man can tame the tongue; it is a restless evil, full of deadly poison. [9] With it we bless our Lord[26] and Father, and with it we curse men who are made in the likeness of God. [10] from the same mouth come both blessing and cursing. My brothers, these things ought not to be so. [17] But the wisdom from above is

---

[23] Max Anders, *Galatians-Colossians*, vol. 8, Holman New Testament Commentary (Nashville, TN: Broadman & Holman Publishers, 1999), 331.

[24] Max Anders, *Galatians-Colossians*, vol. 8, Holman New Testament Commentary (Nashville, TN: Broadman & Holman Publishers, 1999), 225.

[25] Lit., "*nature*"

[26] Gr., *ton Kurion*

first pure, then peaceable, gentle, reasonable, full of mercy and good fruits, impartial, without hypocrisy. [18] And the fruit of righteousness is sown in peace by[27] those who make peace.

3:7–8. Verse 7 mentions four classifications of earthly animals men have subdued or tamed: animals which could walk, fly, crawl, or swim. Genesis 9:2 follows the same type of classification. These classifications represent a human observation about different types of animals rather than a scientific ordering.

Certainly no one has ever tamed a rhinoceros or an alligator, but in general wild animals can be brought under human control. Elephants, charmed snakes, and porpoises are examples of this principle. Although human beings can tame animals, they cannot tame their own tongues. The tongue is **a restless evil,** always busy creating more mischief. We must always keep the tongue under careful guard and never give it freedom to roam relentlessly, for it is **full of deadly poison.** Like the tongue of a serpent, the tongue deals out death (see Ps. 140:3).

Several years ago at the conclusion of a moving musical presentation, a man claiming to be Leonard Bernstein, Jr., son of the world-famous conductor, gave a check for twenty thousand dollars to the sanctuary choir of a large Baptist church. With tears in his eyes the man indicated that he and his father were Christian Jews and members of a New York City Baptist church. He asked that the church use the money to take the church choir to New York to perform with the New York Philharmonic Orchestra. Officials at the bank on which the check was drawn could not locate the account. The office of Leonard Bernstein in New York indicated that he had one son, whose name was Alexander. Neither father nor son had any connection with a Baptist church in New York. Someone had pulled a hoax. He had presented a picture of a tongue full of restless mischief.

The Bible's accurate picture of the tongue's destructive potential offers us no excuse for acquiescing to the tongue's evil potential (see Eph. 4:29). By committing our tongues to the power of God, we can see them used to build up and strengthen others rather than to tear them down.

Recently I spoke to a church in South Texas and focused during one evening on Paul's prayer in Ephesians 1:15–23. I urged my listeners to adopt the requests of Paul's prayer as they interceded for others. The next day one of the members pulled me aside to say that those words from Paul had changed her own prayer life. Her words of encouragement built me up and sent me back to my teaching with

---

[27] Or *for,* or possibly *among*

renewed enthusiasm. A tongue committed to God can be used as a positive tool for building hope and stamina in others.

3:9–10. Verse 9 mentions both a positive and a negative use of the tongue. The positive use involved praise of God, the highest function of human speech (see Ps. 103:1–5). The negative use involved cursing human beings. Cursing refers to personal verbal abuse, perhaps arising from loss of temper in an argument or debate. It also involves the expression of angry wishes on enemies. It includes speech which is insulting as well as profane.

Verse 10 spotlights the inconsistency of this action. We are sinfully inconsistent when we bless God and then curse those made in God's likeness. When we curse those whom God has made, we are effectively cursing God. He is the object of both expressions. Such a double standard is outrageous: **My brethren, this should not be.**

3:17. True wisdom is free from self-interest and strife. This verse lists eight traits or characteristics of true wisdom. The first is purity. People with true wisdom are **pure** in that they have put aside the vices of a self-seeking nature and factionalism. This trait provides the secure foundation for all that follows.

The following five traits show the attitude of true wisdom toward other people. **Peace-loving** means it demonstrates a desire to promote peace between struggling factions. **Considerate** refers to being reasonable in the demands it makes on others. **Submissive** indicates a willingness to learn from others by being open to reason. **Full of mercy** is revealed by offering compassion to those in distress. **Full of good fruit** is shown by kind actions and helpful deeds to others.

The final two traits describe the essential nature of true wisdom in itself. It is **impartial,** without prejudice and unwavering in its commitments. True wisdom is **sincere,** genuine and open in its approaches to others. Jesus particularly showed his genuineness in his dialogues with Pilate (John 18:33–37).

3:18. Verse 18 concludes this section with a description of the effects of true wisdom. True wisdom results in **a harvest of righteousness,** that is, a conformity to God's will. True wisdom also lets one experience **peace,** the enjoyment of harmonious relationships between human beings.

Over the years Christians in various churches have developed wide differences in their social practices. American Christians from the South sometimes oppose mixed swimming, but they may offend a Christian from the North by their cultivation and use of tobacco. Christians differ in their preferences for English versions of the Bible. Some regard the use of certain modern translations as sure signs of compromise and moral apostasy. European Christians live in a culture which more readily accepts the use of alcohol by believers. Many American Christians find it hard to tolerate this acceptance. American women almost never feel compelled to wear a covering for their heads to worship services. Among many eastern European Christian groups it is expected that women will wear a covering, even if it is only a scarf. Each of these circumstances demands a response of peace and consideration to prevent strife, factionalism, and petty quarreling.[28]

Growing Your Humility

It is only possible for you and your wife to communicate in a kind and loving way you are, "humble minded." (1 Pet. 3:8) Humility will get you through the difficulties because it moves you to say, "I'm sorry." At times, the words "I'm sorry" can be more important than the words, "I love you." When you and your wife pray together focus on how you sin against God every day, and yet God forgives you every day, as long as you are truly repentant and remorseful.

Pride will only lead to the ruination of marriage. A proud person is incapable of saying, "I'm sorry, please forgive me." A proud person likes to keep score as to who said what and who started an argument. The proud person likes to make excuses, or blaming another person instead of owning the mistake, rationalizing and justifying. A proud person is not after peace as this one only gets louder trying to rationalize the mistake that led to the argument. (Eccl. 7:9) The proud person will also abandon the conversation because the other person is the one that was wrong, as opposed to saying, "I'm sorry, please forgive me." James tells us, "God opposes the proud, but gives grace to the humble."[29] (Jam. 4:6) Yes, pride will not only ruin a marriage but also your relationship with God.

When you and your wife disagree, it is best to loving and respectfully work to solve the problem quickly instead of being proud, and ignoring the problem. The reason the same problem is never solved and keep rearing its ugly head is, there is never an understanding of what the problem is. Paul said, "Be angry, and yet do not sin;[30] do not let the sun go down on

---

[28] Thomas D. Lea, *Hebrews, James*, vol. 10, Holman New Testament Commentary (Nashville, TN: Broadman & Holman Publishers, 1999), 304-305, 307–308.

[29] A quotation from Pro 3:34

[30] A reference to Ps 4:4

your anger, [27] nor give place[31] to the devil." (Eph. 4:26-27) Going to bed with a heavy heart, to rise in the morning to a distressed mind and spirit, this will cause a separation and a lessening of love eventually. It is best to try and solve the problem quickly in a loving, peaceful, respectful way. If a resolution cannot be met, it is best to hug, hold each other and express your love. This way you go to be knowing all will be well.

> *Ashley Murrell, 33, had [an argument] with her husband Mikey, 36, a carpet cleaner, about his long working hours after he returned home late from a 16-hour shift.*
>
> *The mother-of-three told him to sleep on the sofa after the argument, but when she woke up the next morning, she discovered that he was dead.*
>
> *She later learned that he had been working extra hours to earn enough money to take her to Prague for their wedding anniversary on July 3.[32]*

Good communication is when you and your wife can speak to each other, openly, without fear, honestly but kindly and respectfully about your thoughts and feelings. You have an understanding of your spouse when you truly know how she feels and you meet her needs, as she meets your needs.

---

[31] Or *an opportunity* to the devil

[32] Woman whose husband died after she banished him to the sofa ... https://www.yahoo.com/news/woman-whose-husband-died-banished-sofa-found-love-brother-081433639.html (July 12, 2017)

CHAPTER 7 How to Compromise

Let us say that you and your wife have a different preference on the amount of money that you will spend on a household item. There are only three options to reach a resolution.

First, you can be stubborn until you get you way, or the wife could be stubborn until she gets her own way. **Second**, you could passively submit without discussing or resisting, to your spouse's wishes. **Third**, you and your wife could compromise.

Some feel that compromise is a sign of weakness, which would be a case of pride if you feel that way. Or, others might feel like no one is getting what they want in a compromise.

Understand this comprising need not be a lose-lose situation, but rather it can be done right so that it is a win-win situation. However, before we look at the world of compromising, we need to look at a few things involved in this skill.

What You Need to Know

Teamwork is involved in compromising. It is true; before you were married, you made all of your decisions based on your own view of the pros and the cons of a choice. Now, there is the most important person in the world, who is equally involved in this decision-making process, and you must put your marriage above your personal preferences. This is actually not a negative but rather an advantage. You have likely heard it said, "Two minds are better than one." This is because **two minds have a better chance** of finding the best decision than just one mind alone that may not consider all the evidence. The wife will have insight that you may not have considered and you might have insights that she has not considered.

You must be **open-minded** if the compromise is going to be successful as a win-win situation. Sure, you are not going to agree with everything your wife says or believes, and nor will she agree with everything either. Nevertheless, you have to be truly willing to accept her way, and she has to be truly open to the possibility of your way. If you are sitting there with your arms folded, thinking of rebuttals to everything she says before she even finishes her points, even shaking your head no, there will be no successful compromise.

You must be ready to be **self-sacrificing** if the compromise is going to be successful. You have also likely heard the saying, "it's either my way or the highway." No wife will want to spend her life with the ultimatum, which indicates she will either conform to the desires of her husband or else be excluded. This compromise will only work if both are self-sacrificing, i.e., giving up some things for the other. Marriage is a bit of give and take, not just take.

How to Compromise Correctly

You must begin the conversation by **setting the right tone**, or it will end before it ever begins. If you voice gets louder as you defend your preference, or you resort to harsh words, the likelihood of ending with a successful compromise is very slim. The apostle Paul writes "put on as God's chosen ones, holy and beloved, a heart of compassion, kindness, humility, meekness, and patience." (Col. 3:12) You need to acquire and use such qualities if you and your wife are going to avoid arguing.

Each person should be given the **opportunity to fully explain** why they feel the way they do, without being interrupted, without eye rolling, without the other shaking their head, without the other sitting with their arms folded. Once both have fully explained the reason for their preference, you need to **search for common ground**. Instead of focusing on where your preferences differ, focus in on where they agree.

Finding Common Ground

The two of you need to have a tablet and pen. You and your wife need to make two lists. In the first list, write down the aspects of your choice that you feel most strongly about. In the second list, write down those things that you could give up. After you, both have your list, look them over together, make a list of aspects that you both agree on that you both feel strongest about. Then, work your way through the parts where you both feel you could give ground. The most important thing is having all possible aspects on paper, so you can evaluate more clearly, what can be compromised.

Some issues will be easy to settle, and this process will not be needed. If they are more complex use this process. Also, brainstorm between the two of you to find a solution without having to begin this process. Wise King Solomon wrote, "Two are better than one because they have a good reward for their efforts."–Ecclesiastes 4:9, CSB.

You must have a willing heart that will adjust its view. You must be willing to listen to your wife objectively. Paul Wrote, "let each one of you love his wife as himself, and let the wife see that she respects her husband." (Eph. 5:33, ESV) If both you and your wife truly love and respect each other, you will be willing to consider each other's viewpoint.

Colossians 4:6 Updated American Standard Version (UASV)

Let your speech always be gracious, seasoned with salt, so that you may know how you ought to answer each person.

CHAPTER 8 What Does Subjection in Marriage Mean?

The Christian woman that you marry will have to make many adjustments. The one that might affect her most will touch on her liberty. Before you married her, she was free to make the decisions about her life herself. She need not consult anyone if she did not want. Now that your wife is married, she is now obligated to consult you and get permission on major decisions that she formerly decided. Why is this so?

Because the Creator of humanity created man first and then he created woman as the compliment of the man. He assigned the man the role as the head of the wife and the future children. The feminist today "is a philosophy emphasizing the patriarchal roots of inequality between men and women, or, more specifically, social dominance of women by men. Radical feminism views patriarchy as dividing rights, privileges, and power primarily by gender, and as a result oppressing women and privileging men."[33] This has caused a severe crisis the God-ordained family arrangement of Christians. "Christian feminism is an aspect of feminist theology, which seeks to advance and understand the equality of men and women morally, socially, spiritually, and in leadership from a Christian perspective. Christian feminists argue that contributions by women in that direction are necessary for a complete understanding of Christianity."[34] This is one reason for the high divorce rates among Christian families that we see today. In any organized group of people, from a nation to a family, someone has to have the final decision.

Ephesians 5:22 Updated American Standard Version (UASV)

[22] Wives, be in subjection to your own husbands, as to the Lord.

The apostle Paul here and in verse 23 emphasizes subjection and respect. Yes, a wife is in subjection to her husband but this in no way means that she is inferior to her husband. Every living person in heaven and on earth is subject to someone. It is up to the husband to carry out his headship in a proper manner.

---

[33] Accessed July 12, 2017 https://www.thoughtco.com/what-is-radical-feminism-3528997

[34] Harrison, Victoria S. "Modern Women, Traditional Abrahamic Religions and Interpreting Sacred Texts." *Feminist Theology: The Journal of the Britain & Ireland School of Feminist Theology* 15.2 (2007):145-159.

22 Within the marriage relationship wives[200] are addressed first, and they are urged to be subordinate to their[201] husbands as to the Lord. Although the verse does not contain any verb, 'submit' carries over from v. 21, with the imperative being understood instead of the participle.[202] The notion of submission in the preceding verse is now unpacked without repeating the verb.[203] As we have already seen, the keyword rendered 'submit' has to do with the subordination of someone in an ordered array to another who is above the first, that is, in authority over that person. At the heart of this submission is the notion of 'order'. God has established certain leadership and authority roles within the family, and submission is a humble recognition of that divine ordering. The apostle is not urging every woman to submit to every man, but wives to their husbands. The use of the middle voice of this verb (cf. Col. 3:18) emphasizes the voluntary character of the submission. Paul's admonition to wives is an appeal to free and responsible persons which can only be heeded voluntarily, never by the elimination or breaking of the human will, much less by means of a servile submissiveness.[204]

The idea of subordination to authority in general, as well as in the family, is out of favour in a world which prizes permissiveness and freedom. Christians are often affected by these attitudes. Subordination smacks of exploitation and oppression that are deeply resented. But authority is not synonymous with tyranny, and the submission to which the apostle refers does not imply inferiority. Wives and husbands (as well as children and parents, servants and masters) have different God-appointed roles, but all have equal dignity because they have been made

---

[200] Here the nominative case with the article (αἱ γυναῖκες), rather than the vocative, is used in address (cf. BDF §147[3]). It is 'wives' who are in view, not women generally.

[201] Although the adjective ἴδιος originally signified what was 'one's own', by New Testament times it differed little from a reflexive or possessive pronoun. In this context it is rendered '*their* husbands' (so BAGD, 369; Bruce, 384; Schnackenburg, 246; and Best, 532).

[202] The verb 'submit' does not appear in the best Greek text, so that the verse is dependent for its sense on the participle of v. 21. This is the reading of 𝔓46 B Clement Origen and several Greek mss. according to Jerome. Other textual traditions supply some form of ὑποτάσσειν ('submit') before or after τοῖς ἰδίοις ἀνδράσιν ('their husbands'), such as ὑποτάσσεσθε ('be subject') or ὑποτασσέσθωσαν ('let them be subject'). Most editors argue for the omission of the verb because it is the shorter reading and it is likely that later scribes included the verb for the sake of clarity. For a detailed discussion, see B. M. Metzger, *Textual Commentary*, 608–9.

[203] D. B. Wallace, *Greek Grammar*, 659.

[204] Cf. Barth, 609. M. J. Harris, *Colossians and Philemon* (Grand Rapids: Eerdmans, 1991), 178, comments: 'It is a case of voluntary submission in recognition of the God-appointed leadership of the husband and the divinely ordained hierarchical order in creation (cf. 1 Cor. 11:3–9)'.

in the divine image and in Christ have put on the new person who is created to be like God (4:24).[205] Having described the single new humanity which God is creating in his Son, with its focus on the oneness in Christ of all, especially Jew and Gentile (cf. Col. 3:11; Gal. 3:28), the apostle 'does not now [in this household table] destroy his own thesis by erecting new barriers of sex, age and rank in God's new society in which they have been abolished'.[206] That the verb 'submit, be subordinate' can be used of Christ's submission to the authority of the Father (1 Cor. 15:28) shows that it can denote a functional subordination without implying inferiority, or less honour and glory.[207]

The motivation for the wife to be subject to her husband is spelled out in the final phrase, *as to the Lord.*[208] The general admonition of v. 21 to be submissive in 'the fear of Christ' finds concrete expression for the wife in the marriage situation: as she is subordinate to her husband, so in that very action she is submitting to the Lord. Her voluntary response is not called for because of her role in society, nor is it to be understood as separate from her submission to Christ. Rather, it is part and parcel of the way that she serves the Lord Jesus (cf. Col. 3:23 of servants who engage in wholehearted work for their masters and in that very action serve their heavenly Lord).[35]

Ephesians 5:23 Updated American Standard Version (UASV)

23 For **the husband is the head of the wife**, as Christ also is the head of the congregation,[36] he himself being the Savior of the body.

Again, this verse is not a license to abuse or dominate the wife. It does mean that the husband has the final say in everything as long as he does not require the wife to break God's law. However, only the foolish husband would not consider the insights of his wife. When she is correct, humbly accept her direction. A husband may feel that headship permits him

---

[205] 'Equality of *worth* is not identity of *role*', J. H. Yoder, cited by Stott, 218.

[206] Stott, 217. Note his timely discussion of v. 22 in the light of contemporary attitudes (215–20).

[207] Against the view of G. Bilezikian, 'Hermeneutical Bungee-Jumping: Subordination in the Godhead', *JETS* 40 (1997), 57–68.

[208] 'Lord' (κύριος) is not a reference to her husband, as some have claimed. The plural 'to their lords' (τοῖς κυρίοις) would have been written to correspond to 'to their husbands' (τοῖς ἰδίοις ἀνδράσιν).

[35] Peter Thomas O'Brien, *The Letter to the Ephesians*, The Pillar New Testament Commentary (Grand Rapids, MI: W.B. Eerdmans Publishing Co., 1999), 411–412.

[36] Gr *ekklesia* ("assembly")

to absolute control. However, this is not so. His wife, though in subjection, is not his slave. She is a complement. (Gen. 2:18)

---

23 The reason for the wife's submission to her husband is now expressed through the causal clause: 'for the husband is head of the wife as Christ also is head of the church'. On two earlier occasions in Ephesians the key term 'head' has been used, both with reference to Christ (1:22; 4:15). Now, for the first time, the husband's headship is stated as a fact, and made the basis of his wife's submission. The origin of this headship is not elaborated here, although in the fuller treatments of 1 Corinthians 11:3–12 and 1 Timothy 2:11–13 it is grounded in the order of creation, especially the narrative of Genesis 2 (cf. 1 Cor. 11:8, 9).

In each of the earlier instances of this term in Ephesians it signifies 'head' as 'ruler' or 'authority',[209] rather than 'source',[210] or one who is 'prominent, preeminent'.[211] At 1:22 'head' expresses the idea of Christ's supremacy and authority over the cosmos, especially the evil powers, which he exercises on behalf of the church (cf. Col. 1:18; 2:10). His rule over his people is described at 4:15, and this headship is expressed in his care and nourishment, as well as in his leadership of them in the fulfilment of the divine purposes.[212] Here the headship of the husband, in the light of the usage at 1:22, the general context of the authority

---

[209] So W. Grudem, 'Does *kephalē* ('head') Mean "Source" or "Authority Over" in Greek Literature? A Survey of 2,336 Examples', *TrinJ* 6 (1985), 38–59; and 'The Meaning of Κεφαλή ('Head'): A Response to Recent Studies', *TrinJ* 11 (1990), 3–72. Note the summary of the debate by J. A. Fitzmyer, 'Kephale in 1 Corinthians 11:3', *Int* 47 (1993), 52–59; see also the detailed discussion of G. W. Dawes, *The Body*, 122–49, who concludes that κεφαλή is used as a metaphor indicating 'authority over'. Only in this verse in Ephesians, however, does the term have 'two distinct referents', namely, Christ and the husband.

[210] Advocates of the meaning 'source' include S. Bedale, 'The Meaning of κεφαλή in the Pauline Epistles', *JTS* 5 (1954), 211–15; G. D. Fee, *1 Corinthians*, 502–5; C. C. Kroeger, '*Head*', 267–83; and *DPL*, 375–77.

[211] A. Perriman, *Speaking of Women*, 13–33, who rejects both 'source, origin' and 'leadership, authority over' as meanings for κεφαλή, argues in favour of the term signifying 'prominence' or 'pre-eminence'. He acknowledges that this may 'also entail authority and leadership', but 'it is a mistake to include this as part of the common denotation of the term' (31; cf. Hoehner). This interpretation, however, runs into difficulties with the expression 'Christ is head of the church' (Paul is saying more than that Christ is pre-eminent in relation to the church, though this is true), while his exegesis of vv. 23–24 (55–57) is not convincing. The ἀλλά ('but') in v. 24 does not signify a change of emphasis from headship (v. 23), which only has to do with prominence and preeminence, to subordination with its notions of authority over others. Instead, the adversative ἀλλά ('but') provides a contrast with the preceding clause, 'he himself is the Saviour of the body' (v. 23c), which is not true of the husband's relationship to his wife (see on v. 24).

[212] C. E. Arnold, 'Jesus Christ', 365.

structure of the Graeco-Roman household,[213] and the submission of the wife to her husband within marriage in vv. 22–24,[214] refers to his having authority over his wife; thus he is her leader or ruler.[215]

The mere presence of the terms 'head' and 'submission' in this context does not of itself 'establish stereotypes of masculine and feminine behaviour'.[216] Different cultures may assign different roles for men and women, husbands and wives. What is important here is that the nature of the husband's headship in God's new society is explained in relation to Christ's headship. The husband is head of the wife *as also*[217] Christ is head of the church. 'Although [Paul] ... grounds the fact of the husband's headship in creation, he defines it in relation to the headship of Christ the redeemer'.[218] Christ's headship over the church is expressed by his loving it and giving his life for it, as vv. 25–27 so clearly show. This will have profound implications for the husband's behaviour as head of his wife (v. 28).

The additional words, 'he himself is the Saviour of the body', at first sight appear rather surprising and have caused exegetes to question whether they refer to the husband's role as his wife's protector or are part of the Christ-church/husband-wife analogy, thereby signifying that as Christ is the Saviour of the body, so also the husband is in some sense the saviour of his wife. While the term 'saviour' could possibly be taken in a general sense of protector or provider of the wife's welfare, so that

---

[213] For recent discussions of authority structures in the Graeco-Roman family see Lincoln, 357–59; and Hoehner.

[214] Cf. Lincoln, 369.

[215] Note the discussion of the lexical semantics of this, together with several criticisms of the view that 'head' means 'source', in P. Cotterell and M. Turner, *Linguistics and Biblical Interpretation* (London: SPCK, 1989), 141–45. They conclude that 'head' carries the sense of 'master' or 'lord'.

[216] Stott, 225.

[217] ὡς καί has comparative force, 'as also'. Cf. BAGD, 897; and Hoehner.

[218] Stott, 225. Contra Schnackenburg, 246, who acknowledges that Paul argues from creation in 1 Cor. 11, but considers this argument 'no longer convincing to us'. It loses its status in the light of Christ's headship, expressed in Eph. 5:23b. But if we assume that the 'author' of Ephesians is reflecting a view similar to that expressed in 1 Cor. 11, why should the words 'as Christ is head of the church' overthrow the husband's headship? It is better to speak of the latter being defined or explicated in the light of Christ's headship. K. H. Fleckenstein, *Ordnet euch einander unter in der Furcht Christi: Die Eheperikope in Eph 5, 21–33: Geschichte der Interpretation, Analyse und Aktualisierung des Textes* (Würzburg: Echter, 1994), 216, understands the role of the husband as 'head of the wife' to be derived from 'the patriarchal structure of the ancient family', but does not tie it to creation.

the analogy of Christ's relationship to the church can be parallelled in the husband's 'saving' his wife, both syntax and usage are against it.

Instead, the clause is specifically focussed on Christ, not the husband: the personal pronoun 'he *himself*' is emphatic by its presence and position, and clearly refers to Christ. Nowhere in the context is the wife regarded as the husband's body as the church is Christ's body.[219] Further, the term 'saviour', which turns up twenty-four times in the New Testament, always refers to Jesus or God, but never to human beings.[220] To interpret the words, then, of Christ[221] fits appropriately within the flow of the apostle's argument. Paul has been urging wives to be submissive to their husbands. The reason for this turns on the headship of the husband, which is parallel to Christ's headship or rule over the church. Paul then adds that the person who is head of the church is none other than the one who is the Saviour of the body. His saving activity, especially his sacrificial death (2:14–18; cf. 5:2), was for the deliverance of men and women in dire spiritual peril (2:1–10).

Later in the paragraph, the apostle will urge husbands as heads of their wives to serve them in love. Their pattern is the Lord Jesus, whose headship was demonstrated in his loving the church and giving himself up for it, in order to present it faultless to himself (vv. 25–27).[37]

Subjection Is Relative

The husband authority over his wife is not complete. We can consider the wife's subject to the husband as a Christian is subject to the superior governing authorities. The apostle Paul said, "Let every soul[38] be in subjection to the governing authorities. For there is no authority except by God, and those that exist have been placed[39] by God." (Rom. 13:1) Yet, as Christian, while we obey the laws of the land, it is in conjunction with the

---

[219] The husband and the wife are 'one flesh' (5:31), and husbands are to love their wives 'as their own bodies', but this is a reference to the husbands' bodies, not the wives'.

[220] Of Jesus: Luke 2:11; John 4:42; Acts 5:31; 13:23; Phil. 3:20; 2 Tim. 1:10, etc. Of God: Luke 1:47; 1 Tim. 1:1; 2:3; 4:10, etc.

[221] The suggestions that 1 Cor. 7:16 (with its reference to the believing spouse being the instrument of the unbelieving spouse's salvation) and Tobit 6:18 (where Tobias marries his cousin Sarah to save her) provide significant parallels to the husband being the saviour of his wife have been shown to be unconvincing by Lincoln, 370, and Hoehner. Note the discussion in G. W. Dawes, *The Body*, 150.

[37] Peter Thomas O'Brien, *The Letter to the Ephesians*, The Pillar New Testament Commentary (Grand Rapids, MI: W.B. Eerdmans Publishing Co., 1999), 412–415.

[38] Or *person*

[39] Or *established, instituted*

Word of God. If any governmental authority asked us to do something that breaks God's law, we obey what Peter and the apostles said, "We must obey God rather than men." (Ac 5:29) In a similar way, the wife is in subjection to her husband unless he is asking something of her that is against the Word of God.

1 Peter 3:1-2 Updated American Standard Version (UASV)

3 In the same way, you wives, be submissive to your own husbands so that even if any of them are disobedient to the word, they may be won without a word by the behavior of their wives, [2] as they observe your chaste and respectful behavior.

3:1. These words are addressed generally to all Christian wives, but with special attention to those women whose husbands are not believers in Jesus Christ. **In the same way** takes the reader back to something previously introduced. The manner of behavior is described with the words, **be submissive to your husbands.** Submission appeared first in 2:13 in reference to the believer's response to authority and again in verse 18 in discussing the slave's response to the master.

Opinions vary widely as to how these injunctions should be defined. One well-intentioned but misguided commentator says that "the meaning of the wife's submission to her husband concerns the sexual relationship and should not be taken in a more general and oppressive sense" (Hillyer, 92). Such an interpretation not only violates the meaning of the word but also violates the context of this verse. Submission is best understood as "to voluntarily yield your rights or will to someone else's wishes or advice, as an expression of love for that person." Another spin on the term would be to define it as simply considering the needs of your husband and fulfilling them (Marshall, 99).

In all discussions related to submission, if the wishes, desires, or needs of the husband involve a direct violation of the Word of God, then submission does not apply. In such cases, to practice submission would involve violating the higher principle of obedience to God and his Word previously held out as the believer's goal (see 1:14–15, 22; 2:11).

Submitting oneself to another is the opposite of self-assertion, the opposite of an independent, autocratic spirit. It is the desire to get along with someone else. It involves being satisfied at times with less than what one may deserve or claim as a right. The goal of this type of behavior is to win over to Christ the non-believing husband. This occurs **without words.** This does not mean that a wife is never to speak, but rather that she is not to resort to constant arguments and nagging discussions. The husband will be more influenced by **the behavior** of his wife. This links this chapter to chapter 2, where verse 12 indicates that the non-Christian audience can be positively influenced for Christ as they observe the consistent and godly behavior of a believer.

As Christian wives live out the declaration of the praises of God, their husbands will be influenced. For the Christian wife living with a non-Christian husband, Peter's previous discussion of suffering even while doing what is right may have some application even within the context of her marriage and home. What a Christian wife says often will not change her husband; how she lives out her faith before him will make the difference.

3:2. Living a life of **purity and reverence** can make a difference. Purity signifies more than just moral or sexual purity, although this is included. The term suggests moral and ethical behavior that maintains a high standard. According to recent surveys, forty percent of the women polled by *USA Today* indicated that they have had extramarital affairs. Obviously, Peter's advice is still relevant today. Purity of life will generally not occur, however, unless "reverence" is also a part of it. The "reverence" is for the Lord and indicates a deep desire to keep his commandments. This desire to obey God should be the driving motive, resulting in a high moral standard.[40]

Ephesians 5:24 Updated American Standard Version (UASV)

---

[40] David Walls and Max Anders, *I & II Peter, I, II & III John, Jude*, vol. 11, Holman New Testament Commentary (Nashville, TN: Broadman & Holman Publishers, 1999), 48–49.

24 But as the congregation[41] is subject to Christ, so also the wives should be to their husbands in everything.

> **24** The church's submission to Christ is now presented as the model of the wife's submission to her husband. The exhortation to wives in v. 22 is repeated and reinforced with the addition of the words 'in everything'. Here, however, the sequence of v. 22 is reversed. The analogy of the church being subject to Christ is mentioned before the admonition that *wives should submit to their husbands in everything.*
>
> Although the NIV's introductory *now* does not indicate it, the verse begins with the adversative conjunction 'but', which provides a contrast with the preceding clause, 'he himself is the Saviour of the body' (v. 23c).[222] This is not true of the husband's relationship to his wife. Although he has responsibility for her welfare, he is not her saviour (see on v. 23). So by means of the adversative 'but' (= 'notwithstanding this difference')[223] Paul makes the distinction between Christ and the husband, before comparing the church's submission to Christ with the wife's submission to her husband.[224] By using the same verb 'submit' (a middle voice in the original) the apostle stresses the willing character of the church's submission to Christ, and thus underscores what has already been asserted in v. 22 about the free and voluntary nature of the wife's subordination to her husband.
>
> But what is involved in the church's submission to Christ, and what light does this throw on the wife's submission to her husband? The church's relationship to Christ is the focus of attention in several passages within Ephesians, and these spell out important facets of its submission

---

[41] Gr *ekklesia* ("assembly")

NIV New International Version

[222] So the majority of commentators, including Calvin, Alford, Meyer, Abbott, M. Barth, Sampley, Schnackenburg, Lincoln, and Hoehner. This is better than regarding the ἀλλά as having resumptive ('consequently'; so Robinson, 124, 205; and Bruce, 385) or consecutive force (S. F. Miletic, *"One Flesh": Eph. 5.22–24, 5.31: Marriage and the New Creation* [Rome: Pontifical Biblical Institute, 1988], 102–3). The variations in the English versions ('therefore': AV; 'but': RV, ASV, NASB, NEB; 'and': TEV, JB, NJB; 'now': NIV; or the conjunction was left untranslated: RSV, NRSV) indicate something of the difficulties translators have had in understanding the force of the conjunction (so Hoehner).

[223] Cf. Abbott, 166.

[224] The comparative particle ὡς ('as') begins the comparison, and this is balanced by the adverbial particle οὕτως ('so') and the conjunction καί ('and') which introduce the second clause. Wives (αὐ γυναῖκες) are the subject of the admonition, and the present middle imperative ὑποτασσέσθωσαν ('let them be subordinate') needs to be supplied (A. T. Robertson, *Greek Grammar*, 394).

to its Lord. God has graciously placed everything under Christ's feet and caused him to be head over all for the benefit of the church. The church gladly submits to his beneficent rule (1:22). Christ is the vital cornerstone on whom God's building is constructed. As this new community looks to Christ it grows and progresses to its ultimate goal of holiness (2:20, 21). Christ indwells the hearts of his people, establishing them so that they may be able to comprehend the greatness of his love (3:17, 19). The church receives Christ's gift of grace (4:7), and the ministers he gives for the purpose of enriching the whole body (4:11, 12). The church thus grows towards its head, the ultimate goal of which is the whole measure of Christ's fulness (v. 13), and it receives from him all that is necessary for this growth (vv. 15, 16). In submitting to its Lord, God's people had 'learned Christ': they welcomed him as a living person and were shaped by his teaching (v. 20). This involved submitting to his rule of righteousness and living by standards and values completely different from what they had known. The church is to imitate Christ's sacrificial love (5:2). It seeks to please its Lord (5:10) by living in goodness, holiness, and truth and by understanding his will (5:17). His people sing praises to him (5:19), and live in godly fear and awe of him (5:21). Accordingly, the church's submission to Christ means 'looking to its head for his beneficial rule, living by his norms, experiencing his presence and love, receiving from him gifts that will enable growth to maturity, and responding to him in gratitude and awe'.[225] It is these attitudes that the wife is urged to develop as she submits to her husband.

The additional element which reinforces this exhortation (cf. v. 22) is the concluding phrase, 'in everything'. In the Colossians household table the similar expression 'in everything' is used of the *obedience* of children to parents (Col. 3:20), and of slaves to masters (Col. 3:22; cf. Tit. 3:9). Although this phrase has raised modern questions about the *limitations* of a wife's submission to her husband (arising out of the contemporary desire to control the scope of someone's authority, specifying what decisions a person in authority can make),[226] 'in everything' indicates that the wife is to be subordinate to her husband *in every area of life.* In this sense it is all-encompassing, and is not, as some have suggested, restricted to sexual matters or some other special sphere of their relationship. 'No part of her life should be outside of her

---

[225] Lincoln, 372. Cf. S. F. Miletic, *"One Flesh"*, 43, who aptly comments that 'the Christ/church relationship provides direction ("to the Lord"), perception (husband as "head" as Christ is "head") and example (church as paradigm) for the wife's act of subordination'.

[226] Rightly noted by S. B. Clark, *Man and Woman*, 83.

relationship to her husband and outside of subordination to him'.[227] Just as the church is to submit to Christ in everything, so in every sphere wives are expected to submit to their husbands. The motivation for doing this is a true and godly reverence for Christ (5:21; cf. v. 33).

Furthermore, the exhortation to be subordinate 'in everything' should be read within the flow of the argument in the chapter. By God's design husband and wife are 'one flesh' (v. 31; Gen. 2:24), and the divine intention is that they should 'function together under one head, not as two autonomous individuals living together'.[228] This subordination of wife to husband 'has a practical aspect in that it creates a greater effectiveness in their working together as one'.[229] And it anticipates God's ultimate intention of bringing back all things into unity in Christ (1:10; see below).

The question, then, as to whether the wife is to submit to her husband regardless of what he commands is not addressed. But the words 'in everything', however they are interpreted, are not intended to reverse the instructions and exhortations already laid upon *all* believers in the paraenesis of Ephesians 4–6. This admonition to wives in the household table cannot be interpreted as a kind of grid through which all the earlier exhortations are filtered in the interests of serving the husband's authority.[230] Further, it goes without saying that wives are not to be subordinate in matters that are sinful or contrary to God's commands (cf. Acts 5:29).

There is no suggestion that this exhortation to be submissive is intended to stifle the wife's thinking or acting. She should not act unilaterally, but rather submit willingly to her husband's leadership. 'Just as the church should willingly submit to Christ in all things and, if it does so, will not find that stifling, demeaning, or stultifying of growth and freedom, so also wives should willingly submit to their husbands in all

---

[227] S. B. Clark, *Man and Woman*, 83. If 'in everything' refers to every sphere of the husband-wife relationship, then it confuses the issue to speak of 'complete obedience' or 'full and complete subordination' (as Lincoln, 373, does).

[228] G. W. Knight, 'Husbands and Wives as Analogues of Christ and the Church: Ephesians 5:21–33 and Colossians 3:18–19', in *Recovering Biblical Manhood and Womanhood: A Response to Evangelical Feminism*, ed. J. Piper and W. Grudem (Wheaton, IL: Crossway, 1991), 170. He adds that the wife's 'submission is coextensive with all aspects of their relationship'.

[229] S. B. Clark, *Man and Woman*, 81.

[230] Barth, 620–21, points out that 'in everything' cannot mean mere blind obedience, especially when it would mean acting contrary to God's commands. On the other hand, it is inappropriate to 'compil[e] a short or long list of exemptions to prove that "in everything" actually means "not in everything" ' (621)!

things and, if they do so, will not find that stifling, demeaning, or stultifying'.[231] As with the other admonitions in the household table, God sets forth these instructions for our good.

Accordingly, the wife's submission to her husband is *not conditional* on his loving her after the pattern of Christ's love or showing his unceasing care for her. Later the apostle will make it clear that husbands are not to rule their wives insensitively (vv. 25–27). Those in authority should not 'lord it over' those who are led (2 Cor. 1:24). But the wife's response of submission, which is not an unthinking obedience to his leadership, is to be rendered gladly, irrespective of whether the husband will heed the injunctions explicitly addressed to him or not. Contrary to much contemporary Western thinking, there is no suggestion that wives are to be submissive to their husbands only if their husbands are loving. We have already seen that the church's submission to Christ leads to blessing, growth, and unity for God's people. Similarly, the wife's submission to her husband, as she seeks to honour the Lord Jesus Christ, will *ultimately* lead to divine blessing for herself and others.[42]

THE BASIS OF LOVE

Ephesians 5:22–33

Sometimes, the emphasis of this passage is entirely misplaced, and it is read as if its essence was the subordination of wife to husband. The single phrase, 'The husband is the head of the wife', is quoted in isolation. But the basis of the passage is not control; it is love. Paul says certain things about the love that a husband must have for his wife.

(1) It must be a *sacrificial* love. He must love her as Christ loved the Church and gave himself for the Church. It must never be a selfish love. Christ loved the Church, not that the Church might do things for him, but that he might do things for the Church. The fourth-century Church father John Chrysostom has a wonderful expansion of this passage: 'Hast thou seen the measure of obedience? Hear also the measure of love. Wouldst thou that thy wife shouldst obey thee as the Church doth Christ? Have care thyself for her as Christ for the Church. And if it be needful that thou shouldst give thy life for her, or be cut to pieces a thousand times, or endure anything whatever, refuse it not ... He brought the

---

[231] G. W. Knight, 'Husbands and Wives', 170.

[42] Peter Thomas O'Brien, *The Letter to the Ephesians*, The Pillar New Testament Commentary (Grand Rapids, MI: W.B. Eerdmans Publishing Co., 1999), 415–418.

Church to his feet by his great care, not by threats nor fear nor any such thing; so do thou conduct thyself towards thy wife.'

The husband is head of the wife—true, Paul said that; but he also said that the husband must love the wife as Christ loved the Church, with a love which never exercises a tyranny of control but which is ready to make any sacrifice for her good.

(2) It must be a *purifying* love. Christ cleansed and consecrated the Church by the washing with water on the day when each member of the Church made a personal confession of faith. It may well be that Paul has in mind a Greek custom. One of the Greek marriage customs was that, before the bride was taken to her marriage, she was bathed in the water of a stream sacred to some god or goddess. In Athens, for instance, the bride was bathed in the waters of the Callirhoe, which was sacred to the goddess Athene. It is of baptism that Paul is thinking. By the washing of baptism and by the confession of faith, Christ sought to make for himself a Church, cleansed and consecrated, until there was neither soiling spot nor disfiguring wrinkle upon it. Any love which drags a person down is false. Any love which coarsens instead of refining the character, which necessitates deceit, which weakens the moral strength, is not love. Real love is the great purifier of life.

(3) It must be a *caring* love. A man must love his wife as he loves his own body. Real love loves not to extract service, nor to ensure that its own physical comfort is attended to; it cherishes the one it loves. There is something very wrong when a man regards his wife, consciously or unconsciously, as simply the one who cooks his meals and washes his clothes and cleans his house and brings up his children.

(4) It is an *unbreakable* love. For the sake of this love, a man leaves father and mother and is joined to his wife. They become one flesh. He is as united to her as the members of the body are united to each other, and would no more think of separating from her than of tearing his own body apart. Here indeed was an ideal in an age when men and women changed partners with as little thought as they changed clothes.

(5) The whole relationship is *in the Lord*. In the Christian home, Jesus is an always-remembered, though an unseen, guest. In Christian marriage, there are not two partners, but three—and the third is Christ.[43]

---

[43] William Barclay, *The Letters to the Galatians and Ephesians*, The New Daily Study Bible (Louisville, KY; London: Westminster John Knox Press, 2002), 200–201.

The wife should feel and know that the husband is primarily concerned with her best interest, and will always consider her views, evidencing that he values her voice in all matters. He will make sure that he listens to her and if her view is the correct view, he will wisely follow that course. A husband will demonstrate and express his love and respect for his wife when he carries out his Godly assigned position as the head of the family. (John 13:34) The husband might be imperfect and fallible, but if he follows in the example of Jesus Christ, he will have a wife that loves and respects him as well.

CHAPTER 9 How to Stop Arguing

Does it seem like you and your wife end up in one argument after another? Do you feel like you are walking on eggshells or through a minefield in which any step could cause the spouse to explode?

If this is the case, do not worry because change is possible. You and your wife can make improvements in the way you communicate. However, you and your mate need to discover why arguments keep coming up.

Misunderstandings

Is there a failure to understand or interpret something correctly at times, which leads to a minor disagreement or dispute? Are there times when you say something, and you know what you meant, but the wife reads another meaning into it. Are there times when your wife says she told you something that you were supposed to remember, but you do not even remember her ever telling you?

Differences

There was a couple dating through long distance chat on Facebook. She was from Chile, and he was from America. She spoke Spanish and very little English. He spoke English and next to no Spanish. The cultural difference between two countries over 7,000 miles (11265 Kilometers) removed was a factor as well. Even two people from the same country and even the same city will face differences as to their worldviews. In this case, it is easy to misunderstand based on small or great differences in one's views, culture,[44] languages, and the like.

Bad Examples

Some people's parents argued every day about what seemed like things that were not important or significant. It baffled you as a child at how they argued over the same things year after year, day after day. In these arguments, as things escalated, your parents might have said many disrespectful things to each other. One couple argued every day, almost like clockwork, would say the most heinous things to each other. After a

---

[44] **Culture** is defined as a set of values, practices, traditions or beliefs a group shares, whether due to age, race or ethnicity, religion or gender.

few hours of not speaking to one another, the next thing in the process was a couple of hours of I love you.

Beneath the Surface

Many times, the argument is not even really about what got it started. There is something else beneath the surface, which ignites and fuels an argument. Maybe, you are deep in an argument as to why you are always late! It is not so much about your punctuality as it is your spouse feels as though she is being taken for granted or treated thoughtlessly in a number of things.

Regardless of the cause, frequent arguments have a major impact on a marriage. Not only will it eventually cause the love for each other to cool down, so you grow apart, it will cause health damages as well. Thus, the question, how can you stop arguing?

Steps to fewer Arguments

Why do I say fewer arguments? Before we list what we can do, it is best that we revisit just what our circumstances are as imperfect humans. If a human knows that, they suffer from turrets syndrome, it is no surprise to them or their spouse that they compulsively utter obscenities. Certainly, a wife of a husband or a husband of a wife would not be as troubled by their spouse who utters obscenities because of suffering from turrets syndrome. Therefore, the same married couple should have an understanding of their spouse suffering from inherited sin, imperfections, and human weaknesses, so as to make allowances for falling short. Just how bad is it?

There are four factors to our stress and difficult times **(1)** We are imperfect and live in an imperfect world, compounded by the fact that God's Word says we are mentally bent and lean toward doing bad. We read, "When the LORD saw that the wickedness of man on the earth was great and that the whole bent of his thinking was never anything but evil, the LORD regretted that he had ever made man on the earth." (Gen. 6:5, AT) **(2)** We have a wicked spirit creature, Satan the Devil, who is misleading the entire world of humankind. We read, "Be sober-minded;[45] be watchful. Your adversary the devil prowls around like a roaring lion, seeking someone to devour." (1 Pet. 5:8) **(3)** We live in a world that caters to the imperfect flesh. We read, "For all that is in the world, the lust of the flesh and the lust of the eyes and the boastful pride of life, is not from the

---

[45] **Sober Minded:** (Gr. *nepho*) This denotes being sound in mind, to be in control of one's thought processes and thus not be in danger of irrational thinking, 'to be sober-minded, to be well composed in mind.'–1 Thessalonians 5:6, 8; 2 Timothy 4:5; 1 Peter 1:13; 4:7; 5:8

Father, but is from the world. The world is passing away, and its lusts; but the one who does the will of God remains forever." (1 John 2:16-17) **(4)** We are unable to understand our inner person, which the Bible informs us is wicked: "The heart is deceitful above all things and desperately sick; who can understand it?" The apostle Paul tells us, "just as sin came into the world through one man, and death through sin, and so death spread to all men because all sinned." There is only one major factor in all four parts that will have an effect on the other two, **you.**–Jeremiah 17:9; Romans 5:12.

Yes, at times, we create our own stress. Because **(1)** we do not understand our true imperfection, and our imperfection is easily misled by point number **(2)**, Satan. Moreover, we are easily enticed by point numbers **(3-4)**, the world and its desires, as well as our heart. We read, "But each one is tempted when he is carried away and enticed by his own desire.[46] Then the desire when it has conceived gives birth to sin, and sin when it is fully grown brings forth death." (Jam. 1:14-15, ESV) Only by an active faith in Christ, and a true understanding of our imperfection, can we hope to function in an imperfect world, defeat Satan, gain control over our imperfect flesh, allow God to read our heart and help us **not** to fall victim to our own desires of the eyes? Moreover, many times, it is our imperfect perception of an incident that angers us, not necessarily the spouse.

What Can You Do

If you are serious, you will want to identify the true issue that lies beneath the argument. Just as a noise in a car is not the real problem, it is whatever is lying behind that noise, so too, the argument itself is not the problem. When you and your spouse are getting along, try the following.

Pull out those same two tablets, so that you and your spouse can write down what you believe a recent argument was about. The husband may write, "you were out all day with your friends and **never** called so I would know where you were." Then, the wife writes, "You are **always** angry because I spend time with my friends."

First, we note the absolute thinking errors. **Absolute thinking** is the tendency to think in concrete, black and white terms. "I am absolutely delighted" or "I am absolutely devastated." A cognitive error in which events are interpreted in total or **absolute** ways; thus failure at a particular task might lead to the thought "I cannot do anything right."

Second, consider just how serious the so-called offense was. Is this one of those things that we make allowances for, concerning our spouse because of human imperfection? We have to realize that human imperfection will

---

[46] Or "own *lust*"

64

affect the both of us. In many cases, just agree to disagree. Wise King Solomon said, "Whoever covers an offense seeks love, but he who repeats a matter separates close friends." (Prov. 17:9) Max Anders writes, "When someone has committed an **offense** against you or some third party, you have two options available: cover it over by a discreet silence or publicize it through gossip and complaint. Your choice affects more than just yourself. Covering the offense **promotes love** by maintaining an atmosphere of trust; the person who **repeats the matter** stirs up suspicion, even among **close friends**."[47]

If the matter was insignificant, just apologize, and the other accepts the apology. Then, never bring it up again.

Colossians 3:13-14 Updated American Standard Version (UASV)

[13] putting up with one another and forgiving one another. If anyone should have a complaint against another, forgiving each other; as the Lord has forgiven you, so you also must forgive. [14] And above all these things put on love, which is a perfect bond of union.

On the other hand, if it is a significant wrong, there is another step in this process.

On your tablet, write down what you were feeling during the argument. The husband writes, "I felt as though your friends were more important than me." While the wife writes, I felt like I was being treated like a child and you were my father, whom I had to check in every two hours."

Now, you hand your tablet to your wife and take hers, reading each other's comments. Now, take note of the issue beneath the surface of the argument for each other. Without arguing more, talk about how you felt and what you could (not what the other could) have done differently. Solomon wrote, "A fool gives full vent to his spirit, but a wise man quietly holds it back." (Prov. 29:11) Anders writes, "One of the characteristics of a **fool** is his inability to hold back his anger (literally, his spirit). A **wise man**, on the other hand, keeps his temper **under control**, even in a confrontation. The Hebrew for keeping oneself under control is literally "to calm it back"; the same word is used in Psalms 65:7 and 89:9 to describe the stilling of a storm. What a perfect picture of a godly response when we are tempted to blow up!"[48]

---

[47] Anders, Max. Holman Old Testament Commentary - Proverbs (p. 222). B&H Publishing. Kindle Edition.

[48] Anders, Max. Holman Old Testament Commentary - Proverbs (p. 198). B&H Publishing. Kindle Edition.

Now, take a moment to discuss what you have learned throughout this process. How will it help you to decrease the number of arguments? What was it that each of you truly needs during your dispute, which would have claimed the emotional responses? Was it understanding?

Proverbs 17:9 Updated American Standard Version (UASV)

[9] Whoever covers a transgression seeks love,
   but he who repeats a matter separates close friends.

CHAPTER 10 How to Avoid Hurtful Words

Some spouses enter into a conflict with argumentative tones, and before you know, a flood of hurtful criticism is being hurled at each other. If this grows without finding a way to decrease, it will then become your normal way of communicating with each other. If this is the way of your marriage, you can stop this form of communication. If it has not grown into this pattern of normalcy, you can cut it off at the roots, so that it does not become a norm.

Why Loving People Say Hurtful Words

It should be noted that the godly qualities that our Creator has given us are in every one of us, even in our imperfection. However, we do have another inner desire that wars against our desires to follow the qualities that God has instilled in us. Because of our imperfection, again, we are mentally bent toward evil. (Gen. 6:5; 8:21; Ps. 51:5, AT) Moreover, our heart (inner person, the seat of motivation) 'is deceitful above all things, and desperately sick; which we cannot understand.' (Jer. 17:9) Therefore, if we are going to maintain and develop the quality of putting other people's needs, interests, or wishes before our own, we must cultivate our selfless side. This is especially true within the family because if one person is a selfish person, it will be a life of pain and suffering for everyone else. The reality is, it was the selfishness of Satan, Adam, and Eve that has humankind living in imperfection, pain, suffering, old age, and death. Sadly, every argument between family and friends, every conflict between leaders, every war between nations, every dispute between employer and employee, and every crime is the result of selfishness. Our concern with our own interests, needs, and wishes while ignoring those of others will ruin our life and any relationship we might ever hope to have.

What motivates us to be selfless? It is another human quality, empathy, the ability to identify with and understand somebody else's feelings or difficulties. When we do something for another, like pay for a military person's meal at a restaurant, we are empathizing with what he gave up, so we have the freedom we have. This brings us to another quality, gratitude, i.e., being thankful for what others have done. Imagine, the traffic is moving slowly, and we are laying on our horn because we are in a hurry. Soon, we see several ambulances ahead. As we drive by a car wreck, we see a teenage girl being zipped up in a black body bag. Suddenly, our heart is beating heavily; we feel the pain of that child, the pain of the mother, and our being late for a meeting is the furthest thing from our mind. If we have never pondered whether we carry out selfless acts, we might start with something small. We might focus on getting the door for people, offering better tips for service, helping someone in a small way, considering how others might feel, and seeing how we react to inconveniences. When we see how others react to our small acts of kindness, will help us to develop our selfless side further.

The apostle Paul wrote, "Let each one keep seeking, not his own good, but that of the other person." (1 Cor. 10:24) On this verse, Bible scholar David E. Garland writes, "Paul's command that one "not seek that which is one's own" leaves indefinite what they are not to seek.[3] We can fill in the blank with words such as "advantage," "interest," "good," "ends," "enjoyment," "needs." Instead of selfish things, they are to seek the interests of the other ... This "other" is not restricted to the fellow believer who might have a weak conscience, as in 8:11, but also includes the unbeliever who might offer an invitation to dinner (10:27). His concern in this section is not the effect of their behavior on other believers but its effect on nonbelievers. The overarching hermeneutical principles that govern his practical advice are these: What course of action will bring glory to God, and what course of action will be "the most effective witness to Christ?" (Ruef 1977: 103). Paul expects the Corinthians to do all things to bring glory to God (10:31) and to seek the best interests of others so that they might be saved (10:33)." (Garland 2003, p. 489)

As was stated in the last chapter, some husbands and wives were raised in homes where hurtful words were common among the parents, among the children to the parents, and overhearing the parents talk badly about others. It can be a learned behavior, which can simply be unlearned.

Moreover, we have an entertainment industry today that flourishes with harmful words, the more there are, the bigger the box office sales. Comedians today say the most hurtful things about husbands and wives, as well as children.

In some cultures around the world, men view women as less of a person and feel that real men must dominate their women. In these cultures, if a woman offers her thoughts on something to the mail, it is viewed as challenging the husband, and he looks weak to the other men. In such a culture, family arguments are viewed as being between enemies, not husbands and wives, using hurtful words.

Hurtful words unchecked will eventually lead to a divorce, not to mention the health problem that comes from heated exchanges. Some husbands and wives would say that hurtful words do more damage to the soul that fists do to the body because the body heals, the hurt soul lingers for years to come.

What can you do if hurtful words have already begun to encroach on your relationship with your wife?

What you Can Do

EMPATHY is the understanding of another's feelings: the ability to identify with and understand somebody else's feelings or difficulties. Try not to focus on your pain but imagine what your spouse must be feeling. Walk through arguments that you have had and think of the hurtful words that you have used. Now, ponder how the words must have impacted her. Do not consider what was said or what the argument was about, just the hurtful words that you used and how they must have made your wife feel.

After that, now consider your wife's hurtful words **but make allowances** for your wife's words. Say things to yourself like, maybe she had a past boyfriend that verbally, mentally and emotionally abused her. Does it seem like her words coming from that perspective? Can you understand her reaction is not entirely about you? While it is true that no person should suffer the consequences of another person's past action, it is also true that the wife's actions may be a product of abuse too.

Proverbs 15:1 Updated American Standard Version (UASV)

15 A gentle answer turns away wrath,
   but a painful[49] word stirs up anger.

Max Anders writes, "How can we handle an angry person? Our instinctive response is to come back with a **harsh**, hurtful retort, a tactic that just escalates the level of rage. The other option is a **gentle**, soft **answer**. The wise person can avoid needless quarrels by defusing a tense situation. Such tact requires forethought, patience, self-control, and kindness."[50]

If your life has been the result of parents, who set a bad example with their hard words, you can relearn respect by observing other couples that respect each other. Watch how they interact with each other. The apostle Paul wrote, "Brothers, join in imitating me, and observe those who walk according to the example you have in us." (Phil. 3:17) "Paul's example was Christ. He then lived out the Christ model as he ran the race. He appealed to his readers to follow his example. Some already followed that example, so they, too, serve as models for the Philippians. They had a choice. They could model their lives after those advocating falsehood and fail to win the

---

[49] I.e. *harsh*

[50] Anders, Max. Holman Old Testament Commentary - Proverbs (p. 211). B&H Publishing. Kindle Edition.

prize, or they could model their lives after Christ."[51] Some couples have mastered the Christ model in their relationship; you can imitate their fine example as well.

Hurtful words come from the mind, not the heart or the mouth. The heart and the mouth are just vehicles that carry our thoughts to fruition. It is your perception of things that contribute (not cause) to anger that leads to hurtful words. If you can change your perception, i.e., your way of thinking, you can change how you feel, which will change how you act.

Overcoming Should Statements

We need to come to the realization that nothing or no one is responsible for our anger issues. It is we and we alone. It is common by those that suffer from unrighteous anger to believe; it is the conditions, which cause the outbursts. The truth is nothing can cause us to get angry. However, the events or situations can contribute to our getting angry if we feed them with irrational thinking. When an unpleasant situation falls upon us, we can feel the physical effects of a racing heart, tension in our muscles, the grinding of our teeth, and so on. These physical signs mean that we are dialoguing with ourselves either consciously or subconsciously. Yes, these thoughts can be present in the mind without our awareness of it. It is the physical signs that must wake us up to hidden thoughts.

If you are aware of what you are thinking, because you are saying it aloud, even if it is mumbling under your breath, or you have hidden comments that you are unaware of, you have signs to let you know. You need to be the one to reverse course. You must ask yourself, "What am I saying." Get a grasp of the thoughts that are racing through your mind. Maybe the events are with your spouse. First, we set ourselves up for failure, because the dating stage of a relationship is unrealistic. During this stage, both parties do their best to present nothing but the best side of themselves. After the honeymoon, a few months down the road, both begin to get comfortable and letdown, and show they flawed qualities. It could be a rude awakening, even more so if either of the spouses felt that the marriage was going to be some perfect storybook life, with a happy ending.

If he says she should be like this, or he should be like that, this is another unrealistic aspect. We will get angry if we are caught up in the syndrome of *should*. A Christian marriage should be this way. Life should be like this, or like that. We must realize that we can even do this with

---

[51] Max Anders, *Galatians-Colossians*, vol. 8, Holman New Testament Commentary (Nashville, TN: Broadman & Holman Publishers, 1999), 246.

ourselves as well. "I should do this, or I should do that." When someone or we do not live up to our expectation, this can contribute to frustration. "I should have been paying closer attention." "He should have been more considerate." Generally, we are making these should statement before we are even aware all of the facts.

This *should* syndrome will affect our lives far more than we may ever imagine, contributing to a life of tumult. When we go around setting standards of perfection for others, and ourselves (meaning mistake free), when humankind is imperfect, we are just setting ourselves up for a life of disappointment. We are going to fall short of our own standards that we have set, every day, as an imperfect person. Everyone is going to fall short of our standard setting of what we believe he or she should be like. We expect them to act a certain way in certain circumstances. We expect them to talk a certain way, drive a certain way, react a certain way, live a certain way, believe a certain way, and so on.

When we do not live up to our *should* standards of being mistake free, falling short daily, our statements of "I *should*" are going to contribute to an intense dislike of self, unworthiness and embarrassment, faultfinding, and frustration. When the rest of humanity does not live up to our *should* standards of them, namely being mistake free, we will become hostile toward them, have a self-righteous attitude that they should have done better. Imagine, we are only addressing one word, which possesses so much power, and by changing it, we can free ourselves of constant let downs.

Christians, sad to say, are more susceptible to these *should* statements. Because we are involved in a biblical worldview that revolves around the moral values of God, we tend to begin thinking more of ourselves than we ought to, when we become more successful in our spiritual lives. When we take a pause to notice our should statements, we will see that the vast majority revolve around morality, standards of conduct that are generally accepted as right or wrong. "He should have done a better job in mowing the lawn because I pay him more than enough!" The rational side of that is that there are no rules that the lawn company has to go above the standards for us; he need not take extra pride in his work, just because we think he should. It is perfectly fine to do a standard job, as long as it is not substandard. Another should stamen might be, "He should have thought to call if he knew he was going to be late because it is the decent thing to do!" He probably feels that he should have remembered as well, but he is imperfect, and so is his memory, especially when he is deeply involved in his job.

Our should statements assume that we are entitled to error free people, including ourselves. If we have been "wronged" because of human imperfection, make allowances, forgive them as God forgives us every day.

If we have been wronged because of substandard behavior, take care of it in a rational manner. If we deal with it through anger, we will not get the desired outcome. Rather we will only end up with a defensive person, be it a family member, friend, or another, who may not have had bad intentions to start with, but now he is being pushed into a corner. Think of the folly of this statement, "I was nice to the people at that table, being a good waitress; they should have given me a tip." We cannot be the over someone else's free will, their right to live life the way they believe to be correct. As much as we may desire that they live by our standards, our wanting it will not bring it about.

In fact, if we react inappropriately to what we believe they should or should not do, it will only create bitterness in our stomach, and distance them from us. We certainly detest the idea of anyone taking control of the way we do things, and this is the case with all free-willed people. Once we realize that there is no such thing as absolute fairness among imperfect humanity, as it is relative to the one carrying out the actions. What we see as fair biblically, the world sees as unfair. There is absolute fairness with God, as well as his Word the Bible, but at present, the world of mankind alienated from God do not live by that fairness.

When talking to your spouse, do not say "you did" but rather "I feel" to express your concerns of how things affected you. For example, "**I feel** hurt when you do so many things with letting me know. I worry about you." The other poor choice of hurtful words would be, "That is **just like you, you are** always making plans without checking with me first. Again, Paul said, "Let your speech always be gracious, seasoned with salt, so that you may know how you ought to answer each person."–Colossians 4:6.

Ephesians 4:31-32 Updated American Standard Version (UASV)

[31] Let all bitterness and wrath and anger and clamor and **abusive words** be put away from you, along with all malice. [32] Be kind to one another, tender-hearted, forgiving each other, just as God in Christ also has forgiven you.[52]

Abusive Words: (Gr. *blasphēmia*) This is referring to reviling, malicious talk, abusive words, slander (Matt. 15:19); blasphemy, the content of defamation or slander (Lu 5:21). This is abusive words that are spoken in anger, which could be intentionally or unintentionally hurting another, as well as damaging their reputation.

---

[52] Two early mss read *us*

CHAPTER 11 How to Discuss Problems

At times, when you and your wife are discussing family problems, it starts nice enough but ends with the two of you further removed than when you began. Of course, any learned behavior can be unlearned. Let us consider. As was mentioned earlier, men and women have different ways that they communicate.

As was mention, men are more likely to want to offer quick fixes to the problem, while wives want to talk about the problem in relation to their feelings. Women generally would like to discuss the problem before looking for a solution. They are comforted by being able to express their feelings and know that you, the husband understands them. In some cases, the wife will feel that the talking about the problem is the solution itself. For the woman, she can talk about the problem in minutes and then she is completely over it, while the man tends to ponder what just happened. He might spend the rest of the day thinking nothing got resolved. The husband was not looking for feelings but rather what is the root of the problem and how can we deal with that. He wants to discuss solutions. The fixing of the problem makes the husband feel like progress has been made. This solution-finding mission for the husband is his way of showing the wife he cares and that she can rely on him. He is bewildered at the idea of talking about a problem without talking about the root and looking for a solution.

However, both the husband and wife are right. It takes both talking about the problem and feelings, as well as looking for the root and solving it. The wife needs to express her feeling about the problem, how it impacts her and the husband needs to communicate that he understands her feelings. Then, it is time to move to the root of the problem, followed by solutions. However, you have to be a good listener first. Then the wife needs to be patient as you get your side of things taken care of, so the both of you feel fulfilled.

How to Comfort Your Distressed Wife with Words

Active Listening

Proverbs 20:5 Updated American Standard Version (UASV)

⁵ Counsel in a man's heart is like deep water,
   but a man of understanding draws it out.

Proverbs 18:13 Updated American Standard Version (UASV)

¹³ If one gives an answer before he hears,
    it is his folly and shame.

We need to be able to hear the words that are spoken, as well as the way that it is said, the tone, the body language, so at to get the sense of what is being meant. A common complaint of wives to husbands is that they passively listen to them, blocking out much of what they do not want to hear, because they are opposed, or are not interested in what she is saying. Sadly, we tend to be less appreciative of those who are closest to us than total strangers. Active listening is a form of listening that results in both the speaker and listener having a full understanding of what is meant. There are five points to keep in mind:

(1) **Pay close attention** to what is being said; listen for the ideas behind the words. Do not just hear, but also feel the words. Let the speaker know that you are listening, by leaning forward a little, looking at him, not staring, but having periodic eye contact.

(2) **Look at** facial expression, the tone of the voice, the inflection of the voice, the mood and body language. You want to get at the feelings behind the words. People generally do not say all that is on their mind or convey their true feelings at times, so you have to pay close attention to the non-verbal.

(3) **Turn off your internal thinking** as much as possible. In other words, do not be thinking of how to respond to certain points while he is still talking, because you are going to miss the whole of what he has said.

(4) Let the speaker know **you are paying attention** by nodding from time to time, as well as acknowledging with verbal gestures.

(5) **Reiterate** is not a common word, but it means to repeat what you think the person meant by what they said, but in your own words, to see if you understood correctly. So, you mean … right?'

(6) The person you are speaking with will **acknowledge either you are correct, or he will correct you**, and will restate what they meant, and likely in a more comprehensive way since you misunderstood.

(7) When they have explained their message again, you must **repeat your reiteration.**

Be Empathetic

1 Peter 3:8 Updated American Standard Version (UASV)

⁸ Finally, all of you, have like-minded, sympathy, brotherly love, tender hearted, and humble-minded;

Romans 12:15 Updated American Standard Version (UASV)

¹⁵ Rejoice with those who rejoice, and weep with those who weep.

One of the ways to deal with a challenge is to have empathy. You in your heart must place yourself in their circumstances, getting their mindset. Just because a person comes across abrasively at times, this does not mean that you let them go. There may very well be a reason as to why they are not open to the conversation. This is where insightful, thought-provoking questions, can get at the significant part that has closed them down.

By employing active listening, allowing them to vent, you will understand whatever issues you need to overcome. You might ask, 'tell me, what has you to the point where you are unable to talk this.' This will let them know that you are open to listening. While they are expressing themselves, do not be tempted to resolve their issue, just listen as they fully explain. First, make sure you respond in a calm voice. Then reiterate what they said in a summary point, which will let them know you were listening, and it helps you to know you understand what it is. In the end, you may not agree, but you can empathetically understand in some way.

Be Patient

Psalm 103:14 Updated American Standard Version (UASV)

¹⁴ For he [God] himself knows our formation;
   he remembers that we are dust.

Many times, one has to realize that not every conversation is going to reach a resolution. Therefore, one needs to be patient, and wait for a better time, as it will come up again. Another part of patience is being able to overlook the things the sufferer may say that is hurtful. Recognize that it is the illness speaking, and make allowances accordingly.

Use Your Words Wisely

Proverbs 25:11 Contemporary English Version (CEV)

¹¹ The right word
   at the right time
   is like precious gold
   set in silver.

Proverbs 15:23 Updated American Standard Version (UASV)

²³ A man has joy in the answer of his mouth,
   and a word in season, how good it is!

Use your words to strengthen the depressed one, help him or her to see their good qualities. Be specific in your praises. Let them know that the problems that you face together, the troubles of the past, and time when you both have fallen short are not reflective of the good person he or she is.

CHAPTER 12 How to Solve Problems

Some husbands struggle to control their anger. Then, the husband and wife might have disagreements about different family situations. Then, there is a breakdown in the communication. As this author keeps reminding the reader, you need to keep reminding yourselves; no marriage will ever be perfect. This is no fairy tale where everything works out just fine all the time. However, it will have a happy ending.

Proverbs 18:19 Updated American Standard Version (UASV)

[19] A brother offended is more unyielding than a fortified city,
   and there are disputes like the bars of a fortress.

In looking at the historical setting of this verse, Max Anders tells us, "Conquering an opposing army in the open field was always easier than gaining a fortified city. In fact, one reason Joshua asked God to lengthen the day during the battle at Gibeon was to enable him to destroy the enemy armies before they could reach the safety of their home cities (Josh. 10:11). An invading army could try to climb the walls, demolish the walls or gates with a battering ram, build a ramp to the top, or dig tunnels underneath. If such efforts failed, the enemy would simply surround the city and wait for water and food supplies to run out. This, however, could take years. The Assyrians besieged Samaria for three years (2 Kgs. 17:5), and the Babylonians camped around Jerusalem for eighteen months (Jer. 52:4)."[53]

This principle behind proverb is related to the marriage in that, over time, if you do not resolve the problems of marriage, these problems might be "like the bars of a fortress," which block communication altogether. Therefore, you need to open the door of effective communication

What It Takes for Effective Communication

Matthew 11:28-30 Updated American Standard Version (UASV)

Jesus' Yoke Is Refreshing

[28] "Come to me, all you who are laboring and loaded down, and I will give you rest. [29] Take my yoke upon you and learn from me, for I am

---

[53] Anders, Max. Holman Old Testament Commentary - Proverbs (p. 238). B&H Publishing. Kindle Edition.

gentle and **lowly in heart**, and you will find rest for your souls. [30] For my yoke is easy,[54] and my burden is light."

Yes, if we are going to be an effective communicator, we must learn from Jesus. What do we learn from Jesus? First, Jesus is "gentle," which is the English for the Greek word *praus* that is found "three times in Matthew and once in 1 Peter ... means 'gentle, humble, considerate, meek in the older favorable sense' (BAGD)."[55] In what sense was Jesus, "lowly in heart"?[56] With his knowledge and understanding, as the Son of God, he could have taught in Jewish schools, having some of the greatest Jewish minds as students. He could have taught the Jewish teachers themselves if he so desired.

However, Jesus chose to teach the lowliest of the Jewish world, from the seaside, fishermen. He lived and taught among the poor and the low in social position. It is a privilege to pattern ourselves after such a teacher as he was. This humility and lowliness of heart qualified him as the greatest teacher ever, so it will qualify us, as he teaches us, to be teachers of others. When we are lowly in heart, following in the footsteps of Jesus, we too will refresh our wife. A husband who is gentle, humble, considerate, meek, will bring comfort to his wife. The wife with a receptive heart will find you refreshing, respecting you in your conversations all the more.

In Acts 20:19, it says that the Apostle Paul served the Lord "with all humility," with "humble-mindedness" or "humility of mind." The Greek (*tapeinophrosune*) literally reads "lowliness of mind."[57] It is derived from the words *tapeinos*, which means to "make low," "lowly, "humble" and *phren*, "the mind." Paul told the Philippians that they were to "do nothing from selfish ambition or conceit, but in humility **["lowliness of mind"]** count others more significant than yourselves." (Phil. 2:3-4) Paul also told the Corinthians, "Let no one seek his own good but the good of the other." (1 Cor. 10:24) This quality of "lowliness of mind" will stop you from assuming a superior attitude or tone when you speak to your wife.

---

[54] I.e. *easy to bear*

[55] Leon Morris, The Gospel According to Matthew, The Pillar New Testament Commentary (Grand Rapids, MI; Leicester, England: W.B. Eerdmans; Inter-Varsity Press, 1992).

[56] The heart ([kardia]) is the core and center of man's being, the mainspring of dispositions as well as of feelings and thoughts. It is the very hub of the wheel of man's existence, the center from which all the spokes radiate (Prov. 4:23; cf. 1 Sam. 16:7). All of this also applies to Christ's human nature.—William Hendriksen and Simon J. Kistemaker, vol. 9, Exposition of the Gospel According to Matthew, New Testament Commentary (Grand Rapids: Baker Book House, 1953-2001).

[57] W. E. Vine, Merrill F. Unger and William White, Jr., vol. 2, Vine's Complete Expository Dictionary of Old and New Testament Words, 314 (Nashville, TN: T. Nelson, 1996).

Additionally, if you want to be effective in your communication, one must follow Paul's counsel found at Colossians 4:6,

Colossians 4:6 Updated American Standard Version (UASV)

⁶ Let your speech always be gracious, seasoned with salt, so that you may know how you ought to answer each person.

Certainly, patience and tact, which is skillfully expressing yourself when your wife's feelings are involved, are two qualities that establish effective communication. When you communicate with your wife, your words must be in good taste. Good speech will keep lines of communication open, but unwise, foolish, and careless comments will close those lines of communication.

If you are prepared to talk to your wife you will not be anxious but will be relaxed, which will have a calming effect on your wife, too. However, allow your wife to do most of the talking, to get at the heart of their thinking and feelings. You can never understand your wife's thinking because if you do not know what is going through her mind. For example, your wife could make a comment, and you could choose a phrase and give several minutes of feedback, which proves to be irrelevant to what she meant. It would have been better to ask, "What do you mean by …?" Once she explains herself, then you can offer your thoughts.

Loving Communication

The characteristics of being gentle, humble, considerate, meek, modest, lowliness of mind, tactfulness and patience make the qualities of a good communicator. When you also has selfless love, you will become a great communicator.

Matthew 9:36 Updated American Standard Version (UASV)

³⁶ When he saw the crowds, he had compassion for them, because they were **harassed** and **scattered**, like sheep without a shepherd.

Mark 6:34 Updated American Standard Version (UASV)

³⁴ When he went ashore he saw a great crowd, and he had compassion on them, because they were like sheep without a shepherd. And he began to teach them many things.

"**Harassed** is from a verb meaning to trouble, distress. **Scattered** is from a verb meaning to throw down. The past tense used here implies the thoroughness of their oppression and its persistent effect on the people.

These people were completely and perpetually discouraged."[58] The Jewish religious leaders of Jesus' day did next to nothing in offering enough to make common people feel pleased or content in their spiritual hunger. Rather, they made their lives even more burdensome with all of their rules and regulations that they tacked on to the Mosaic Law. (Matt. 12:1, 2; 15:1-9; 23:4, 23) The religious leaders revealed their true heart condition when they said about those listening to Jesus, "this crowd who does not know the law is accursed!" (John 7:49) Jesus' selfless love moved him to "find rest for their souls," getting on the road to life. Today, you as the loving husband have the mind of Christ that is filled with love as well, and you must offer love to your wife in a selfless way, too.

1 Thessalonians 2:7-8 Updated American Standard Version (UASV)

[7] But we became gentle[59] in the midst of you, as a nursing mother tenderly care for[60] her own children. [8] So, being affectionately desirous of you, we were well-pleased to impart to you not only the gospel of God but also our own souls,[61] because you became beloved to us.

2:7. Instead, Paul and Silas chose to be **gentle**. There is no tenderness quite like a mother's, and Paul dared to identify with maternal love and care. Greek writers used the term *gentleness* to describe those who dealt patiently and with a mild manner toward those who were difficult—obstinate children, unmanageable students, those who had not reached maturity and were experiencing the inconsistencies and struggles of development. Whatever difficulties the Thessalonians may have presented, Paul and Silas recognized that these new Christians were not yet "grown up." So rather than dealing with these people in an authoritarian manner, they chose to be patient—like a mother.

It is a great lesson for the church today, because we have not always been patient with new or young believers. Sometimes we have cut a mold and demanded that they fit it—now. Instead of this approach, we need to see each individual's need for help and encouragement as he or she struggles to conform to the image of Christ.

2:8. Here is a classic understanding of biblical love. To Paul, love is always a verb, it is doing. Feelings may accompany love, but they do not define it. Instead, the commitment of acting in the best interest of

---

[58] Stuart K. Weber, vol. 1, Matthew, Holman New Testament Commentary, 130 (Nashville, TN: Broadman & Holman Publishers, 2000).

[59] Some MSS read *babes*

[60] Or *cherishes*

[61] Or *lives*

another opens the way for feelings: **We loved you so much that we were delighted to share ... our lives.**

It is easier to teach theology than to love, easier to share lists than time. Paul gave not only the message of the gospel, but the example of it as well. He spent time. He shared joys and headaches. Parents and teachers, coaches and mentors, pastors and leaders know what it means to give part of their heart away to others. Love is not just a job. It is a way of life.

But note that Paul did *share* the gospel of God. He was balanced. He gave his life and love. He gave content as well. It is not enough to visit people in the hospital or prison, or to show compassion to the poor or those new in the faith. Somewhere, carefully and candidly, they must also hear the truth of the cross and what it means to trust and follow Christ.

Arguing whether the church should meet people's physical needs or whether it should limit itself to preaching the gospel is like debating which wing of an airplane is more important. Both are essential![62]

The Apostle Paul started numerous congregations, one right after the other, from Antioch of Syria, throughout Asia, into Macedonia, down through Greece and Achaia. The apostle Paul was like a father to thousands of Christians. What made Paul such an effective evangelist? Was it his zeal for spreading the Good News? Yes! The above says that Paul was "**affectionately desirous**" of the new Thessalonian congregation. "Here is a classic understanding of biblical love. To Paul, love is always a verb, it is doing. Feelings may accompany love, but they do not define it. Instead, the commitment to acting in the best interest of [your wife] opens the way for feelings: **We loved you so much that we were delighted to share ... our lives.**"[63] The love Paul had for God, and his neighbor made him a successful evangelist.

If your wife repeatedly rejects your communication, this is a sign of poor communication skills. Have you done your best to be an effective communicator with your wife, when any opportunity presents itself? If you answered yes, and she still has felt troubled or hurt during your communication times, you might want to consider the qualities of Jesus and Paul in the above text. Do an isolated study of what those words mean.

---

[62] Knute Larson, *I & II Thessalonians, I & II Timothy, Titus, Philemon*, vol. 9, Holman New Testament Commentary (Nashville, TN: Broadman & Holman Publishers, 2000), 23–24.

[63] Knute Larson, vol. 9, I & II Thessalonians, I & II Timothy, Titus, Philemon, Holman New Testament Commentary, 24 (Nashville, TN: Broadman & Holman Publishers, 2000).

Then, start focusing on one at a time, seeing how you can use it in your daily life.

Four Steps to Solving Problems

(1) Do not just start talking about a major problem. Find a good day and time to discuss the issue. This will allow both of you to ponder your approach. You might want to set a regular time each week that is set aside to discuss family problems. Try to find that day and time where both are less stressed.

(2) Allow your wife to express her feeling and talk openly about the problem, while you respectfully listen. Keep in mind; you are not looking to win some battle between you and her.

(3) Then, once she has completely finished, you need to acknowledge what she has said, reiterating it, and letting her know you fully understand her feelings. Do not reuse her words when you repeat her sentiments back to her. Say it in your own words, telling her what she has said and how she feels. Never assume that you know what she means. Ask if she has said something ambiguous.

(4) Find common ground and agree on a solution. Marriage is a team, both needs to work together.

A husband and wife that fail to work together as a team will end up with a failed marriage. Then again, if you work together, there is no problem that cannot be resolved.

CHAPTER 13 How to Show Respect

Respect in a marriage is not an option, it is necessary. Men, in particular, innately need respect. Again, Paul says, "let each one of you love his wife as himself, and let the wife see that she respects her husband." (Eph. 5:33, ESV) While you need to respect your wife, God created man in such a way that he actually flourishes on respect. Men feel good knowing that they can handle things for the family, solving the problems. When your wife respects you for such capabilities, it benefits the both of you.

Ponder for a moment, what are the three main things that you admire about your wife? These qualities move you to respect your wife. For the next couple weeks, keep an eye on yourself, watching what you say, and how you say it.

Proverbs 12:18 Updated American Standard Version (UASV)

[18] Thoughtless speech is like the stabs of a sword,
    but the tongue of the wise is a healing.

On this verse, Anders writes, "Fools hurt others with **reckless words**, but the **wise** person heals others with carefully chosen words. In this case, the speaker may not intend to cause harm, but he blurts out his mind without thinking through the consequences. The verb from which "reckless" is derived is used to describe the hasty words that cost Moses his entrance to the land of Canaan (Ps. 106:33). And though there may be no malice, the damage can be as searing as **a sword** thrust. A wise person has the chance to come along afterward and use his **tongue** to help heal the wound."[64] Do you truly speak respectfully to your wife? How often in a week do I find things to complain about as opposed to things to praise her about. When you are complaining what is the tone of your voice. If you asked your spouse about your answers, would she agree? Make it your goal to compliment your wife in the morning after work, and before you go to sleep. Also, try to take note of all the ways she makes your life better. Over time, it will become natural to express your love.

Colossians 3:13 Updated American Standard Version (UASV)

[13] putting up with one another and forgiving one another. If anyone should have a complaint against another, forgiving each other; as the Lord has forgiven you, so you also must forgive.

---

[64] Anders, Max. Holman Old Testament Commentary - Proverbs (p. 220). B&H Publishing. Kindle Edition.

Ponder three ways that you can show respect for your wife.

CHAPTER 14 The Wife's Dignified Role In the Marriage

God created Adam first, then Eve. Adam had spent some time in the garden before the creation of Eve, gaining some experience in living as a new creation. During this period, God gave Adam some instruction. (Gen. 2:15-20) Being the first to be created, Adam was to take the lead in this new family arrangement. His initial role was his informing Eve about the things he had learned from God before her creation, such as the eating from the trees.

Today, the Christian congregation is the same. The apostle Paul wrote, "I do not permit a woman ... to exercise authority over a man, but to be in silence. For Adam was formed first, then Eve." (1 Tim. 2:12-13) This does not mean that the woman cannot talk in the Christian congregation. She is to be silent as in not challenging the authority of men by belittling his lead over the congregation, nor to teach the congregation. This does not mean that she cannot teach the Sunday school for the children or even a Bible study group for women. However, the primary teaching of the Christian congregation is the men's responsibility alone.

The apostle Paul offers us insights into the role of men and women when he wrote, "For man is not from woman, but woman from man. For indeed man was not created for the sake of the woman, but woman for the sake of the man. This is why the woman ought to have a symbol of authority on her head, because of the angels. Nevertheless, in the Lord neither is woman separate from man nor is man separate from woman. For just as the woman is from the man, so also the man is through the woman; but all things are from God."–1 Corinthians 11:8-12.

Looking back at the Law given to the Israelites rights, freedoms, and was treated with honor. They could show their ability to act on your own and make decisions without the help or advice of their husband. Proverbs 31:10-31 speaks of "An excellent wife" who with her own hands gladly makes clothes for the family. Why she even makes clothes to sell to the shop owners. (Verses 13, 21-24) She is like a sailing ship that brings food from across the sea. (Verse 14) She knows how to buy land and how to plant a vineyard. (Verse 16) She knows when to buy or sell, and she stays busy until late at night. (Verse 18) She helps the poor and the needy. She takes good care of her family and is never lazy. (Verses 20, 27) Thus, the wife was shown respect and praised in public for what she had done. – Verse 31.

The opportunity for women to make spiritual progress existed under the Mosaic Law. In Joshua 8:35, we read, "There was not a word of all that Moses had commanded that Joshua did not read aloud in front of all the congregation of Israel, **including the women** and children and the foreign residents who were living among them." In the book of Nehemiah, we read about Ezra, "So Ezra the priest brought the Law before the congregation of men, **women,** and all who could listen with understanding, on the first day of the seventh month. And he read aloud from it before the public square in front of the Water Gate, from daybreak until midday, to the men, **the women,** and all who could understand; and the people listened attentively to the book of the Law. (Neh. 8:2-3) The women under Israelite Law benefited from the reading of God's Word. The women enjoyed these reading and benefited from the wisdom the same as the men did.

Then, we move to the days of Jesus, where we find several women tending to the needs of Jesus, playing an important role in his ministry. (Lu 8:1-3) While the men treated Jesus with disdain, we find one woman that saw Jesus as so special, "a woman with an alabaster jar of costly perfumed oil approached him, and she began pouring it on his head as he was dining," anointing Jesus. (Matt. 26:6-13; John 12:1-7) It was a woman, namely, Mary Magdalene, who was the first person that Jesus appeared to after his resurrection. (Matt. 28:1-10; John 20:1-18) After Jesus had ascended back to heaven, there were 120, who met in the upper room to pray, which included **"the women** and Mary the mother of Jesus, and his brothers." (Acts 1:3-15) That means that there were women in the upper room on the day of Pentecost 33 C.E., when "they were all filled with the Holy Spirit," and many spoke in a number of different languages. – Acts 2:1-12.

It was both men and women who were among those that experienced the prophecy of Joel 2:28-29, as the Apostle Peter quoted it. He said, "I will pour out my Spirit on all flesh, and your sons and your daughters shall prophesy ... and even on my male slaves and on my female slaves I will pour out some of my Spirit in those days, and they will prophesy." (Acts 2:13-18) In the first century and into the beginning of the second century C.E., women were favored with the gifts of the Spirit. They spoke in foreign languages and prophesied. Note that prophesying does not necessarily mean making predictions because the Greek word (*propheteuo*) also means to proclaim the Word of God., i.e., sharing Scriptural truths. In his letter to Christians in Rome, the apostle Paul speaks affectionately of "Phoebe our sister," recommending her to them. He writes, "I commend to you our sister Phoebe, a minister of the congregation at Cenchreae." (Rom. 16:1) What does the word "minister" mean to the modern-day reader?

Servant, Minister: (*diakonos*) The term can refer to one who holds the position of deacon within a Christian congregation, but the term does not necessarily mean that because the Bible uses the word *diakonos* in a broader sense, as one who waits on or attends to the needs of others. (Matt. 20:26; Rom. 16:1; Eph. 6:21; 1 Thess. 3:2) It is also used in the broad sense of those who witness to unbelievers, sharing Scriptural truths, for the purpose of converting them to the faith. (Rom. 16:1-2, 12; Phil. 4:2-3) When Paul refers to "our sister Phoebe, a minister of the congregation at Cenchreae," he is not talking about a religious leader, male or female, who presides over a congregation. Women in the first century had no position of authority within the Christian congregation as an elder (overseer) or deacon (minister, servant). They served as ministers in that "these women, [were ones] who struggled alongside [Paul] for the gospel" (Phil. 4:2-3), as well as many others to grow the Christian faith from 120 disciples in 33 C.E., to over one million disciples by 130 C.E. They were ministers in the sharing of the gospel.

A Christian sister can minister in many ways today. She can be used to carry out Sunday school classes for the children, to run a Bible study for women in the congregation, to share biblical truth within her community to grow the congregation. We also have many female Christian apologists today, who defend the faith, the Bible, and God himself. Some of these have become Christian apologist authors, like Judy Salisbury. Women have also played a major role in the missionary field as well.

If man and woman develop and grow their roles within the Christian congregation, as well as in the marriage, it will bring them happiness. It is when one or the other goes beyond the Word of God, trying to usurp a position that is not theirs to be had, we find conflict. Yes, the modern-day feminist movement and liberal and moderate Christianity have twisted the scriptures to try to make the Bible say things that it does not. The apostle Peter tells "some things [are] hard to understand [in Paul's letters], which the untaught and unstable distort, as they do also the rest of the Scriptures, to their own destruction." (2 Pet. 3:15-16) Conservative Christian women, some with bachelor's degrees, master's degrees and even doctorates in religious education do not alter the Word of God for the sake of modern feminism. The husband too does no go beyond the Scriptures, but rather he exercises his headship, not in a selfish way, but in a loving way. – Ephesians 5:25-33.

A Christian wife 'should have deep respect for her husband.' (Eph. 5:33) Max Anders writes, "**Respect** (*phobetai*) literally means "fear." It can refer, however, to the fear a person should have before God, a reverence and respect (Luke 1:50; 18:2; Acts 10:35; 1 Pet. 2:17; Rev. 14:7; 19:5). This type of reverence and regard should characterize the relationship of a wife and her husband."[65]

Peace and harmony succeed, overcome, and conquer when men and women carry out their God-given roles. This results in their happiness and delight. Moreover, obeying with Scriptural requirements clothes the husband and the wife with the self-respect associated with an honored place in God's family.

---

[65] Max Anders, *Galatians-Colossians*, vol. 8, Holman New Testament Commentary (Nashville, TN: Broadman & Holman Publishers, 1999), 173–174.

CHAPTER 15 What Does Wifely Subjection Mean?

Ephesians 5:22 Updated American Standard Version (UASV)

²² Wives, be **in subjection to your own husbands,** as to the Lord. ²³ For **the husband is the head of the wife,** as Christ also is the head of the congregation,⁶⁶

As we can see in the above, the Word of God clearly states at Ephesians 5:22, "Wives, be **in subjection to your own husbands,** as to the Lord." What does it mean to be in subjection? Must a wife slavishly submit to every demand from her husband, regardless? Can she never act on your own and make decisions without the help or advice of her husband? Can she never think for herself, or believe differently from her husband?

In order to answer these questions, let us look at a Bible account of a woman, Abigail, who acted wisely when she went against her husband, Nabal. David was God's chosen king of Israel. The people of Israel and King David showed great kindness to Nabal. Yet, Nabal addressed them angrily and screamed at them, when King David made a request. King David did not take this well, he was going to deal harshly with this Nabal. Abigail realized how she, her husband and the whole household were in grave danger. She got King David to turn back from his anger.–1 Samuel 25:2-35.

Abigail admitted to David that her husband was a worthless man. She then helped David and his men out with the provisions they had asked for, which Nabal had withheld. Now, under normal circumstances, a loving wife should never publicly say something demeaning about her husband. Was Abigail wrong in speaking poorly of her husband? No, in this instance, she was saving her life, the lives of those in the house, and the life of her worthless husband. There is nothing in God's Word, which shows outside of this one time; Abigail made it a practice to talking badly about others. The account is also clear that Nabal did not complain about how Abigail handled things. However, in this situation, Godly wisdom meant that she needed to act on her own, making the decision, without the help or advice of her husband. Lastly, the Bible praises Abigail for her actions. – 1 Samuel 25:3, 25, 32-33.

Discernment Needed

---

⁶⁶ Gr *ekklesia* ("assembly")

It is not a good thing for a wife to feel as though she is pressured to do anything that is unwise or contrary to God's Word, simply because she is in subjection to her husband. In addition, she should not be made to feel guilty for taking the initiative in some essential matter, as was true of Abigail, not to mention Sarah with Abraham, in the case of Hagar and Ishmael.—Genesis 21:11-12.

The wife being in subjection to her husband is not an absolute obligation that she must comply with everything her husband says. How do we determine the difference? When the right principles are at stake, she may choose to disagree with her husband. However, this is no license to reject everything he says because the wife is falling back on this Scriptural principle here (bypassing the husband out of willfulness, spite, or other wrong motives). It is similar to the license to drive. As a licensed driver, you obey all the traffic laws. The laws gave you while you are on the road. But if a child walks out in front of you, you would choose to swerve so as to miss the child, even if it meant breaking the traffic laws, like going into the other lane or driving up on the sidewalk. This freedom, liberty to ignore the traffic laws in such an incidence does not give you the right to start ignoring minor traffic laws as you see fit. Lastly, even on the occasions when you show initiative or choose to disagree with your husband, you still do so in a godly manner.

The Husband Who Ignores His Headship

Under the direction of God's Word, it is the wife's goal and spirit of subjection that she cooperates with her husband, supporting the decisions that he makes. This is not burdensome if her husband is a spiritually mature Christian. If he is not, it can be a challenge.

If the husband is spiritually immature, how can the wife deal with this? Until the husband rightly assumes his role as the head of the house, she can offer her insights as suggestions on how to benefit the family. It is as though she is steering the relationship and slowly letting him take over the driving as he becomes more skilled in his role as the husband. However, continually nagging the husband would not be in line with the wife's biblical subjection. (Prov. 21:19) However, if the husband's poor decision is putting the family in jeopardy in any way, she may choose to follow the course that keeps the family safe.

Then, there is the wife who is married to the unbeliever, which raises the wifely subject to an even greater challenge. Nevertheless, she should remain in subjection as long as the Word of God is not being violated and the family is in no sort of jeopardy. If the husband does ask her to violate God's Law, she would, "obey God rather than men."—Acts 5:29

Even wives and husbands that feel they have a good understanding of Scripture, both can overstep their role within the family at times. The husband may lack concern and thoughtfulness in his decision making; the wife may press too hard to have her own way. How can they avoid this? It is by developing the quality of selflessness, where they do not put too much emphasis on self, as "we all stumble many times."–James 3:2.

Most men are very appreciative of a wife who shows initiative if it is done thoughtfully. Also, the level of cooperation is improved if both apologize when they make fall short due to human imperfection. We must remember how many times a day we sin against God, and he forgives us readily each time we ask.–Psalm 130:3-4.

CHAPTER 16 Is There Anything Wrong with Flirting

Flirting is behaving in a playfully alluring way through words or actions that you are romantically interested in a person of the opposite sex. Is it wrong for you to show another that you are romantically interested in them? Not really, like most things, it all depends on your intentions. If you are interested in another romantically, it makes sense that you have to make your intentions known, if you are going to know if they feel the same.

However, flirting just when you have no romantic intentions toward another would be wrong. There are young popular persons in your school, who get most of the attention. However, even they have that someone that they are attracted too, secretly wishing the feeling were mutual. How would this popular person, who, on the surface, seems to get everything he or she wants, feel if that other person flirted with them, getting their hopes up, and they are not really interested all? It is fine to give someone special attention because you do want a romantic relationship. However, it only causes pain and hurt to toy with someone's feelings, leading him or her on, and then pull the rug out from under him or her because you were never serious.

Why do some people flirt with others when they have no romantic intentions? Some are only concerned with their own exaggerated sense of self-importance. These ones know that everyone is interested in them, which causes a power trip where they crave the attention. This is an act of callous disregard for the other person's feelings. The empty-headed like to treat life and others as their plaything. You should seek to do what is right.

The Dangers of Flirting

Flirting will ruin their reputation in the end. Yes, there is an immediate satisfaction from their crowd of friends. However, in the end, it will catch up with them because treating others like crap for entertainment will only be funny for a very select heartless few. If the person flirting for entertainment, having no real interest, continues down this path, he or she will discover that ninety-nine percent of the school will see them as disgusting. Love cares more for others than for self. Love doesn't want what it doesn't really want. Love doesn't walk around arrogantly looking for attention, it isn't full of themselves, it doesn't show flirtatious interest on others with no intentions, it is not always thinking of itself.

Flirting will hurt the person you flirt with. There is not one young person who would ever want to be flirted with by a person, who is just seeking attention for himself or herself. Almost none would want to be around a person, who is flirty. They know that the only reason the flirt is even speaking to them is that it is a game. You see, in the end, no one takes a flirt serious because he or she could never really know his or her true intentions. Once a person has a reputation as a flirt, it is very difficult to undo. Try to do what is good for others, not just what is good for you. Think, have you ever thought for even a moment that someone was romantically interested in you? Then, you discover that you were wrong. The feeling is very painful and if things like this happen enough, it can lead to your not being able to trust anyone.

Flirting will destroy any hope of having genuine romance. Who would want to marry a person that has the reputation of being a flirt? Who would want to date a person that has a reputation as a flirt? How could you ever trust a flirt? He or she is seen talking one on one with someone of the opposite sex, the first thing in your mind is, complete suspicion that he or she is flirting. Moreover, how could you ever know if he or she truly loved you? You should never spend time with people who lie. You should never keep company with pretenders. Let me add a note to these last two thoughts. All of us have lied. Some of us have lied because it seemed like the right thing to do to avoid embarrassment or something that would hurt another. All of us have pretended in a relationship; try to be the best person we can. On a small scale, these are harmless to a degree. It is when a person is a malicious liar, having a desire to cause harm or pain to another for recreational purposes or even evil intentions. Flirts are not attractive people.

When a person flirts, they hurt people, who then tell others what type of person you are. The more you flirt, the further the word will spread, until one day; you have no one to flirt with, and no one to date romantically. If you do not stop with the flirting, you might as well prepare yourself for a lonely life of isolation.

CHAPTER 17 Avoid The Pitfalls of Immorality

What can Christians do to stay safe in such an influential world that caters to the fallen flesh? We might have thought that a book, like Proverbs that is 3,000 years old would be out of date on such modern issues, but God's Word is ever applicable. King Solomon in Proverbs chapter 5 will give us the answers we need. However, it is up to us to follow the counsel.

INTRODUCTION

Pay Attention to the Father

Proverbs 5:1 Updated American Standard Version (UASV)

5 My son, be attentive to my wisdom;
   incline your ear to my understanding,

My son, be attentive to my wisdom: The Hebrew (*qā·šăḇ*) **be attentive** means to listen and pay attention, to give heed. In other words, it means that you accept the information that you are given as true and then favorably respond to it. **Wisdom:** (Heb. *ḥāḵ·mā(h)*) is sound judgment, based on knowledge and understanding. It is the balanced application of that knowledge to answer difficulties, achieve objectives, sidestep or ward off dangers, not to mention helping others to accomplish the same. The wise person is often contrasted with the foolishness or stupid person. – Deut. 32:6; Prov. 11:29; Eccles. 6:8.

Incline your ear to my understanding: The Hebrew (*nā·ṭā(h)*) **incline** is when one leans their ear in the speaker's direction so that they can hear better. This is simply a more literary way of saying be attentive or pay attention. The believer needs to carefully listen to the Father and heed his words. **Understanding** (Heb. *tᵉḇû·nā(h)*) is the ability to see how the parts or aspects of something are connected to one another. One who possesses understanding can see the big picture (the entire matter) and not just the isolated facts. – Prov. 2:5; 9:10; 18:15.

Like many of the other chapters in the book of Proverbs, it begins with the plea for the son to heed his father's wisdom. Immorality is likely the greatest pitfall for any young man. Thus, Solomon takes this issue up five times in the first third of Proverbs. (2:16-22; 5:3-23; 6:24-35; 7:5-27; 9:13-18) If the young man or woman for that matter is to avoid falling into immorality, he or she will need to pay attention to wisdom, the ability to apply Bible knowledge, and listen to understanding, the ability to see into a given situation, so as to ascertain right from wrong.

Thinking Ability to Protect You

Proverbs 5:2 Updated American Standard Version (UASV)

[2] that you may keep discretion,[67]
   and your lips may guard knowledge.

That you may keep discretion: The phrase **discretion** (i.e., thinking ability) has been used in 1:4; 2:11; 3:21. In all four verses, the phrase is referring to the ability to make wise choices as well as use good judgment. **Discretion (thinking ability):** (Heb. *mezimmah*) In the evil sense, this can mean wicked plans, evil ideas, schemes, and devices. In the favorable sense, it can mean shrewdness, perceptiveness, discretion, and prudence. In the favorable sense, it is the ability to judge wisely and objectively. *Mezimmah*, therefore, the human mind and thoughts can be used for an admirable and upright end, or for evil purposes. – Ps 10:2; Pro. 1:4; 2:10-12; 5:1-2.

And your lips may guard knowledge: The **lips** (*śā·p̄ā(h)*) here, which is serving as a protection, guarding or watching over our **knowledge** is being contrasted with "the lips of a forbidden woman" in the next verse. In other words, your lips should be filled with wise words that will serve as a protection in contrast to the flattering lips of an adulteress.

In order to possess the good sense or the good judgment and the sensibility needed to avoid what we will label as innocent appearing situations, that is, it seems innocent enough, but it is really a dangerous situation that can lead to ultimate downfall; the young one needs to see where there may not even be evidence that there is seduction in the air.

An older woman may use cunning, smoothness, and crafty ways to slip into the affections of an inexperienced young man in the ways of the world. Being innocent, the young man may not perceive her charms. Once he is seduced, he may still find it difficult how he fell into the disgraceful situation that brought about this ultimate wrongdoing. Many young men have lost themselves to the seductive woman, being sexually exploited.

Beware of a Smooth Lips

Proverbs 5:3 Updated American Standard Version (UASV)

---

[67] Or *thinking ability*; the ability to give wise and careful attention (study) of a matter, based on accurate or full knowledge

³ For the lips of a strange woman drip honey,
  and smoother than oil is her mouth,

For the lips of a strange woman drip honey: The (*zār*) **strange woman** (2:16) is referring to those who set aside what was in harmony with the Mosaic Law and thus distanced and estrange themselves from God. Therefore, the immoral sensual woman (prostitute) was not necessarily a foreigner. "The strange woman," the prostitute, is described as one "who forsakes the companion of her youth" (2:17), which is referring to the husband of her young womanhood. She has ignored and disregarded the prohibition on adultery that was a part of **the covenant of her God**, the Mosaic Law covenant. (Ex. 20:14) Solomon uses the sweetness of (Heb. *nō·p̄ēṯ*) **honey** (the sweetest substance in the ancient world and the smoothest substance in the Israelite home) to illustrate the temptation to sexual immorality that the "strange woman" can bring to bear (achieve) by her appeal to a man with her use of beauty, sexual attraction, and smooth words. It is a fine warning to Christians today.

And smoother than oil is her mouth: Her (Heb. *ḥēk̲*) **lips**, the contributing factor to the young man's downfall, were used as a figure of speech, in reference to her words. The Hebrew word *zarah* rendered **"stranger"** here in this context was a reference to a woman that had left the Law, who is now a prostitute or an immoral woman. In this Proverb, like is true of most seductresses throughout history, it is not her physical beauty alone, but primarily the sound of her voice and her words that lead the young man astray. Again, **honey** is the sweetest substance in the ancient Israelite home and is compared to her words. Verse 3 uses the sweetness of honey to illuminate the enticement to sexual immorality that the **strange woman** (forbidden woman) will wield by her entreaty to a young man with her seduction of flattering and smooth words, **smoother** than oil.

You Can Remain Chaste in an Immoral World

Proverbs 5:4-5 Updated American Standard Version (UASV)

⁴ but in the end she is bitter as wormwood,
  sharp as a two-edged sword.
⁵ Her feet go down to death;
  her steps take hold of Sheol;

But in the end she is bitter as wormwood: What initially seemed so sweet and appealing will only end as bitter as (Heb. *lă·ʿᵃnā(h)*) **wormwood**, a leafy plant that yields a bitter-tasting extract. In Scripture, among other things, wormwood is compared to the aftereffects of immorality.[68]

Sharp as a two-edged sword: This encounter has the possibility of making one ill, in severe pain, and even leading to death like a **two-edged sword**. This brief encounter of sexual immorality will feel like you are being slashed with a two-edged sword, which at the very minimum will cause you emotional wounds and pain.

Her feet go down to death: That one sexual encounter can lead to death might seem highly unlikely, until the age of seeing the world through the internet. Sexually transmitted diseases, such as AIDS, Syphilis if not treated can cause **death**, certain types of HPV[69] can cause cervical cancer, which if not caught can end in death, Gonorrhea and Chlamydia can cause sterility if not treated; in addition, it can lead to PID[70] which again, if untreated can cause death. Hepatitis B can lead to a debilitating disease and over time failure of the liver. This is all in the age of extraordinary science. Can we imagine in the Ancient Near East, with no medication to treat diseases? Then, death can also come from a spouse that is betrayed and acts out in rage to take the life of the two violated the marriage bed.

Her steps take hold of Sheol: The seductress's steps lead to (Heb. *šᵉʾôl*) **Sheol**, which is a transliteration of a Hebrew word that refers to the grave of humankind. The wisdom here would be in taking a moment, to think of the outcome of one's actions, as opposed to the momentary pleasure of immediate gratification.

A distressed inner-self, an unexpected child, a disease transmitted through a sexual encounter, or the breakup of a home, all bitter results of

---

[68] Wormwood is also compared to the bitter experience that came upon Judah and Jerusalem at the hands of the Babylonians. (Jer. 9:15; 23:15; Lam. 3:15, 19) It also represents the suffering as the result of injustice and unrighteousness (Am 5:7; 6:12) and is used with reference to apostates. (Deut. 29:18) At Revelation 8:11, wormwood indicates a bitter and poisonous substance, also called absinthe.

[69] Human Papilloma Virus

[70] Pelvic Inflammatory Disease

an immoral indiscretion. In addition, let us consider the massive emotionally distraught spouse, who may never be able to trust you again because of your unfaithfulness. It only takes one act of betrayal to alter the course of multiple lives for generations.

She Lures Her Prey Off the Path of Life

Proverbs 5:6 Updated American Standard Version (UASV)

⁶ she does not ponder the path of life;
   her ways wander, and she does not know it.

She does not ponder the path of life: Unlike wisdom, the strange woman does not (Heb. *pā·lăs*) **ponder**, examine or weigh, pay attention or scrutinize, give careful thought or consideration to the **path** that she is traveling.

Her ways wander, and she does not know it: Rather, she is (Heb. *nûꜟ*) **wondering** without any destination, aimlessly through a life of immorality, not even **knowing** the end consequences. In other words, through shear ignorance, she has sidestepped the path of life. Does this sound like the person we should allow to seduce us? Her ignorance is willful rejection of wisdom, and so we should not be deceived by feeling sorry for her. She is the predator, not the prey.

Her entire objective is to lure her prey off the path of life. There is only one path to eternal life and that is a marriage commitment to one mate for life, which she has refused to travel. Rather, she has willfully chosen the path of sexual immorality and worse still, she has purposely chosen to be a temptress, to drag others down this path that leads to Sheol, death.

The Believer's Path Is Far Away from the Immoral Path

Proverbs 5:7-8 Updated American Standard Version (UASV)

⁷ And now, O sons, listen to me,
   and do not depart from the words of my mouth.
⁸ Keep your way far from her,
   and do not go near the door of her house,

And now, O sons, listen to me: After a section of giving his sons counsel about their unrealistic nature of ideas or desires about the strange woman's suggestion of underlying passion and sensuality, the father enters into another plea for his sons to **listen** (Heb. *shama*), that is pay attention and obey, never departing from his words.

And do not depart from the words of my mouth: The Hebrew for **put away** (*sûr*) from (4:24) meant to remove something concrete or abstract, to take it away, to cause it to go away. Here, the same Hebrew word (*sûr*) has the meaning **depart**, leave, that is, to make a movement **away from** the words of the father and the path of the righteous, life.

Keep your way far from her: The sons' **way** (*dĕ·rĕḵ*) or path of righteousness (life) is another route, which is different from the strange woman, that is, the immoral woman. The Hebrew **far** (*rā·ḥăq*) is to be a great distance from another. The sons' path of righteousness is certainly far removed from the immoral path of the strange woman. **Her** is the strange woman from verses 3-6.

And do not go near the door of her house: Passing by the door of her house may seem innocent enough but is really a dangerous situation that can lead to ultimate downfall. The son needs to see where there may not even be evidence that there is seduction in the air. Verse 8 has it contrasted as to the sons warning to keep themselves far from her and do not go near.

The sons need to stay as far away as possible from the door of temptation, the fleshly influence of the strange woman. There is no reason to take the risk of listening to her raspy voice, seeing her sensual figure, exposing them to her immodest clothing. How foolish to place human senses, seeing, hearing, and smelling, in the presence of temptation.

Bringing this counsel into the twenty-first century, we need to keep **far away** from all immoral influences, whether they come through a person or immoral music, entertainment, the internet, or even books and magazines.

Keep Your Way Far off from the Wayward Person

Proverbs 5:9-10 Updated American Standard Version (UASV)

⁹ lest you give your honor to others
  and your years to the merciless,
¹⁰ lest strangers take their fill of your strength,
  and your labors go to the house of a foreigner,

Lest you give your honor to others: Is there not a lack of (Heb. *hôḏ*) honor (reputation and self-respect) on the part of the young man, who gives his body, mind and heart in the prime of his life, to one who is merely using him for her pleasures? Is it not shameful to seek out immediate gratification, or the selfish passions of another?

And your years to the merciless: He will lose his **years** (early death or spent unwisely) to a woman who not only has no mercy (Heb. *ʾăḵ·zā·rî*) for him but is also cruel in her ruthless pursuit of him. The blindness of his passion will cause him to not see the losses he is about to suffer because of following his physical desire.

Lest strangers take their fill of your strength: He will lose his (Heb. *kōᵃḥ*) **strength** (honor, physical health, sexual vitality, and self-worth). He will lose his **labors** (cost of adulteress). Bible scholar Longman states, "The point of these verses is clear: The price of infidelity may be high, for everything one has worked for, position, power, prosperity, can be lost either through the avaricious demands of the woman or the outcry for restitution by the community."[71]

The Immorally Erring Believer

Proverbs 5:11 Updated American Standard Version (UASV)

¹¹ and you groan at your end,
    when your flesh and body are consumed,

and you groan at your end: To (Heb. *nā·ḥăm*) groan is to indicate vocally in an inarticulate way pain, discomfort, or displeasure. You were in such a rush to feed your fleshly desires, and now you **groan** over the pain and suffering that has resulted, such as sexually transmitted diseases. **At your end**, does not necessarily mean the end of your life, but rather the end of the affair with the strange woman.

When your flesh and body are consumed: Here the (Heb. *bā·śār*) **flesh** and (Heb. *šᵉ'ēr*) **body** is referring to the literal body of flesh and muscles, the physical body or the whole person, we well as your personality and being. Any sexually transmitted disease will **consume** (Heb. *kā·lā(h)*) and hasten the deterioration of an already imperfect body. This would also be the case of being consumed with shame, guilt, anxiety and the stress or worry of being caught.

Besides the disease and pain that you may bring upon his own **flesh and body** when you turn to immorality, the possible disease and pain upon your wife who is one flesh with you, and upon your future children, you also bring disunity, a suspicion that will plague you for life, and a lack of peace into his married life. But worse than this, you bring yourself to a spiritual death in that you leave the path of life and enter on the path that leads to death. You pay the price of having God's disapproval, whose eyes have been upon your ways and paths.

I Have Paid a High Price

---

[71] Longman III., Tremper; Garland, David E.; Ross, Alan P., vol. 6, Proverbs - Isaiah, The Expositors Bible Commentary, Rev. Ed., 78 (Grand Rapids: Zondervan, 2008).

Proverbs 5:12-13 Updated American Standard Version (UASV)

¹² and you say, "How I hated discipline,
  and my heart despised reproof!
¹³ I did not listen to the voice of my teachers
  or incline my ear to my instructors.

And you say, "How I hated discipline: Here **hated** (Heb. *sane*) has an emotion ranging from disliking intensely, abhor, detest, loathe, open hostility, antipathy or aversion towards a person or thing, but in other places it can have the weaker *sense* of being "set against," also being toward a person or thing. **Discipline** (Heb. *mû·sār*) is repeatedly mentioned throughout the book of Proverbs. In the Scriptures, discipline often carries the sense of correction, admonition, rebuke, or chastisement. It is the practice or methods of teaching and enforcing acceptable patterns of behavior: correction, admonition, or modification, whether it is self-discipline or the discipline of another. According to *The Expositor's Bible Commentary*, it "denotes the training of the moral nature, involving the correcting of waywardness toward folly." (Garland and Longman 2008, 48) Do we need this training? Whether we are disciplining ourselves, or are being disciplined by another, by grasping the counsel within the Scriptures, and then applying it in our lives, it moves us to become a better servant of God. If we are to move over from inherited death to life, we need discipline. – Prov. 1:3; 3:11; 5:12

And my heart despised reproof: Here the Hebrew term (*nā·'ăṣ*) for **despise** has the meaning of looking down on with contempt, to scorn, reject, spurn, strong dislike, which matches **hatred** from line 1. Here **reproof** (Heb. *tô·kă·ḥăṯ*) has the sense of an act or an expression of criticism or disapproval, even condemnation. It is speaking strong words of disapproval, which may also include punishment. – Ps 39:12; Prov. 1:23, 25, 30; 3:11; 5:12; 6:23; 10:17; 12:1; 13:18; 15:5, 10, 31, 32; 27:5; 29:1, 15; Ezek. 5:15.

I did not listen to the voice of my teachers: The Hebrew term (*shama*) means to **listen**, to hear, to pay close attention, and respond, heed, or obey on the basis of having heard. In other words, you did not obey the words of the instructions from the teacher or you did not pay attention to the words of the teacher.

Or incline my ear to my instructors: The Hebrew (*nā·ṭā(h)*) **incline** is when one leans their ear in the speaker's direction so that they can hear better. This is simply a more literary way of saying be attentive or pay attention. You need to carefully listen to the instructor and heed his words.

Regret is all you have left, so you start in with the "only If" or "why did I not." You ask yourself, why did I reject corrective counsel? Why did I not listen to my teachers? Why did I not take instructors words seriously? Why did I allow the strange woman to have her way with me? Why have I ruined my life? It is all too little too late, as I have failed to heed the voices of reason and logic. My life has been one of regret where had I listened to the teachers and instructors instead of stubbornly discarding their counsel, life would not have been one disaster after another. Now, late in life, my conscience has condemned me and my long hatred for the instructors and teachers is regretful. I have failed to obey my teachers, my instructors, and my father.

The Dishonorable Marriage

Proverbs 5:14 Updated American Standard Version (UASV)

[14] I am at the brink of utter ruin
in the assembled congregation."

I am at the brink of utter ruin: The Hebrew (*rǎ'*) **ruin** is literally "in all evil." The sense for the term here is a calamitous event, which resulted in a great loss and misfortune. Here the young man has been so inundated with foolish behavior that he has now become the victim one can suffer: dishonor, disgrace, terrible public shame, even possibly death. Under the Mosaic Law, some sexual immorality could lead to the death penalty. Under the law of Christ, the penalty for unrepentant sexual immorality is total, eternal destruction, death.

When one lives life to the world's idea of the fullest extent of looking for nothing more than one avenue of pleasure after the other, it will eventually come to the "if only" syndrome. **If only** I had listened to my father, to the teachers, to the instructors. **If only** I had taken other paths in life. **If only** I had paid attention to the wise advice I had received. However, this is too little too late because this foolish one who sought pleasure, immediate gratification above all else had ruined his life and his reputation is stained. It is vital that we ponder the high price of sexual immorality before we are immersed by it!

In the assembled congregation: The two words **assembled** (Heb. *qā·hāl*) and **congregation** (Heb. *'ē·ḏā(h)*) mean the same thing, a group of people who are gathered together, usually for religious purposes. In this case, it is the community of this man, who have gathered together to examine his sexually immoral offenses.

Immorality or sexual misconduct can seem like the greatest thing in the beginning, until it becomes public knowledge. The family, the community, and the congregation now know, and your shame is unbearable, you are in utter ruin!

Enjoy Your Marriage

Proverbs 5:15 Updated American Standard Version (UASV)

¹⁵ Drink water from your own cistern,
  flowing water from your own well.

Drink water from your own cistern: The Bible is not squeamish about sexual relations, and we do well to follow that example, if we are to help, our young ones avoid the pitfalls of this world. The **cistern** (Heb. *bôr*) or **well** is an underground tank for storing *precious* rainwater and is being used as a poetic expression for the *precious* wife, who satisfies the desires of her husband. This is considered a private water source, unlike the water supply in public places. Therefore, the point is quite clear, just as you drink water from *your own* cistern or well, you only have sexual relations with *your own* wife.

Flowing water from your own well: Having sexual pleasure with one's wife is compared to drinking refreshing water from *your own* well. This comparison may not resonate with many in our modern world, but ancient Palestine had a dry climate that left them waterless at times. Moreover, they had to dig wells to seek out water, so it was a very precious staple of life. This figurative language instructs the husband to have sexual relations only with his wife. Just as the precious water of the arid climate of Palestine from the husband's own well brought physical life to the husband, so to sexual intimacy from his wife brought pleasure to his life.

Sexual Satisfaction Is not to Be Sought Outside Marriage

Proverbs 5:16 Updated American Standard Version (UASV)

¹⁶ Should your springs be scattered abroad,
  streams of water in the streets?

Should your springs be scattered abroad: Springs (Heb. *mă'·yān*) refers to a natural flow of groundwater that comes to the surface, which flows from beneath the ground, and should be distinguished from water that is stored in a well or a cistern. **Scattered abroad** means to be thrown or moved, spread far from the place from which it originated.

Streams of water in the streets: Streams translates a word (*pĕ·lĕḡ*), which refers to a natural body of water that flows on or underground within the bed and banks of a channel.

Both **springs**, as well as **streams**, are regularly used in the Old Testament as a means of enjoyment or pleasure. However, the **cisterns** and

wells spoken of in verse 15 are located on the property of the owner, while the **streams** and **springs** of verse 16 are often at a distance.

Just as the "cistern" of verse 15 stood for the wife's sexual affections for her husband, the "springs" and "streams of water" of verse 16 is a reference to the husband's sexual affections for his wife.

In other words, verse 16a would read something like, 'shall your [the husband's] springs [sexual affections] be scattered outward [someone other than his wife]? Verse 16b would read, 'in the streets [where prostitutes are], shall there be streams of water [the husband's sexual affections]?' Verse 15-16 gives the reader an analogy that the "cistern" [the wife] satisfies the sexual desires of the husband, and the "springs" and "streams of water" [the husband] satisfies the desires of the wife.

Using figurative language, the Scriptures employ the terms **cistern** and **well** of verse 15 and **springs** and **streams** of verse 16 as expressions of "water sources" to denote a source of the wife's sexual affections for her husband in verse 15 and to denote a source of the husband's sexual affections for his wife in verse 16, with the point being made that sexual satisfaction is not to be sought outside of the marriage. Of course, the love between husband and wife properly involves the marital relationship. However, all those outside the marriage must be excluded from its intimacies.

Forbidding Any Kind of Unfaithfulness in the Marriage

Proverbs 5:17 Updated American Standard Version (UASV)

¹⁷ Let them be for you alone,
and not for strangers with you.

Let them be for you alone: This verse replicates and reinforces the command in verses 15–16. The pronoun **them** (Heb. *hā·yā(h)*) is a reference to the "cistern" and "well" of verse 15 and the "springs" and "streams" of verse 16, which are used to denote a source of the wife's sexual affections for her husband in verse 15 and to denote a source of the husband's sexual affections for his wife in verse 16. In other words, the water sources (sexual affections) of your household are for you alone and should not be shared with others.

And not for strangers with you: Stranger: (Heb. *zār*) was applied to those who forsook what was in harmony with the Mosaic Law and so were estranged from God. Thus, at Proverbs 2:16, the one morally estranged harlot or prostitute is referred to as a "strange (Heb. *zār*) woman." (Prov. 2:16; 5:17; 7:5) The point being made here is simple, do not share your sexual affections with another.

Sexual intimacy should be for you and your spouse alone, which like life saving-water, it should not be wasted on strangers. May the sexual desires that the husband receives from his wife and the wife receives from her husband, be his and hers alone, never to be shared with another. These verses, 15-17, are forbidding any kind of unfaithfulness in the marriage, even flirting.

Take Sexual Satisfaction (Pleasure) In the Wife of Your Youth

Proverbs 5:18 Updated American Standard Version (UASV)

[18] Let your fountain be blessed,
  and rejoice in the wife of your youth,

Let your fountain be blessed: A fountain (Heb. *mā·qôr*) is a well, a fountain, a natural spring of groundwater, which is a relatively small body of water either on the surface of the ground or just below the ground, which denotes the sense of life and cleansing associated with clean and pure water. (Prov 5:18; 25:26; Jer. 2:13; 17:13; 51:36; Hos 13:15; Zech. 13:1) Here the meaning of **your fountain** is the husband's wife, who is the source of his sexual affections. **Blessed** (Heb. *bā·rǎk*) refers to God blessing the husband. It is God pronouncing good or showing favor, having favorable circumstances or state at a future time, for the husband who has a righteous standing before God because of his having remained faithful to the wife of his youth, as he has never had sexual relations with anyone other than his first wife, either by committing adultery or by finding a manufactured reason for divorcing your first wife. Happiness and being highly favored by God characterize this rejoicing in your wife.

And rejoice in the wife of your youth: The meaning of **blessed** from line one is seen in the parallel word in the second line of our verse, "and **rejoice** (Heb. *śā·mǎḥ*) in the ..." Both **blessed** and **rejoice** are referring to the husband who is content, full of joy because of his wife, who is the source of his sexual affections. This text is emphasizing the sexual affections within a marriage, as has been the case since verse 15. The Hebrew *samach* is *a command* to **take sexual satisfaction (pleasure) with your first wife,** which infers that the husband should never look for or seek sexual relations outside of the **wife** of his **youth,** which is speaking of the young age when they were married, i.e., the first wife. The marriage should embrace sexual satisfaction, joy, and contentment.

May the husband's sexual desires continue to be quenched by the wife of his youth, not in seeking out a second wife, a mistress, or a prostitute? God will certainly bless, i.e., bring happiness and rejoicing in the sexual satisfaction between a husband and the wife of your youth but not in any other relationship with any other person.

Husbands Be Intoxicated with Satisfaction in the Pleasures of Your Wife's body, Love, and Affection that She Gives You

Proverbs 5:19-20 Updated American Standard Version (UASV)

¹⁹ a loving doe, a graceful mountain goat.
Let her breasts satisfy you at all times;
    be intoxicated always in her love.
²⁰ Why should you be intoxicated, my son, with a strange woman
    and embrace the bosom of a foreigner?

A loving doe, a graceful mountain goat: The wife is described as "a loving doe, a graceful mountain goat." (Prov. 5:18-19) Solomon was an intelligent observer of the wildlife in Israel, so unquestionably he had a good reason for using this metaphor. To the husband, who has allowed his passions for his wife to continue over the years, she is as desirable and attractive as a female deer, and he is intoxicated with the pleasure she continually brings him, with her body and her love. The husband should reciprocate this to her and her alone. Solomon "characterizes the wife of his youth as a doe or graceful deer, terms that are erotic and reminiscent of Song of Songs 2:9, 17; 8:14."[72]

The female wild goat has to be tough as well as graceful. As God made clear to Job, the wild mountain goat gives birth in the mountainous peaks and bluffs, in rocky, remote and difficult places where food may be rare and temperatures are brutal. (Job 39:1) Notwithstanding these difficulties, she takes care of her offspring and teaches them to climb and leap among the rocks as gracefully, swiftly, and agilely as she does. The wild goat also bravely and fearlessly protects her young from predators. It is nothing to see a female wild goat fighting an eagle for great lengths of time, as her young kid hides beneath her for protection.

Women of God, who are wives and mothers, they oftentimes must raise their children under unfavorable conditions. Like the wild female mountain goat, they show commitment, devotion, and unselfishness in caring for their God-given privilege that is a very heavy responsibility at times. And they courageously endeavor to protect their children from both physical and spiritual dangers. So, Solomon was not belittling women with

---

[72] John H Walton, *Zondervan Illustrated Bible Backgrounds Commentary (Old Testament): The Minor Prophets, Job, Psalms, Proverbs, Ecclesiastes, Song of Songs*, vol. 5 (Grand Rapids, MI: Zondervan, 2009), 476.

this metaphor, rather he was actually bringing attention to a woman's grace and beauty, her spiritual qualities that radiate through even in the most difficult conditions. In this context, the Hebrew word (*chen*), translated **graceful**, means 'grace or elegance of form and appearance that is attractive and draws interest from her husband, pleasing, and stimulating him.'

Let her breasts satisfy you at all times: Here in this context (Heb. *dăḏ*) **breasts**, a sexually desired area of the body should be taken as a symbol or image of love, affection, or charm. NJPSV[73] translates literally: "Let her breasts satisfy you at all times." John H Walton writes, "The wish that the son might be intoxicated by his wife's breasts and inebriated [intoxicated] by her love is also paralleled in the Song of Songs, where the woman claims that the man's 'love is better than wine' (Song 1:2, 4; 4:10). Love and lovemaking make one lightheaded, similar to the effects of drinking wine."[74]

Be intoxicated always in her love: The Hebrew word (*shaga*), which is rendered **intoxicated**, is generally used in reference sin that is committed unintentionally, like our innocent appearing situation that we have spoken about throughout Proverbs chapter five. On reference work reads, "The primary emphasis in the root [*shaga*] is on sin done inadvertently. This is indicated in several ways. First, the two derivatives from [*saga, shegia*, and *misgeh*] indicate an act perpetrated in ignorance, not willfully. Second, in the ... The Scripture pinpoints at least three causes for such wandering. The first is wine and strong drink (Isa 28:7; Pro. 20:1). The second is the seductive strange woman (Pro. 5:20, 23) versus the love of one's wife, which ought to 'captivate' one (Pro 5:19). The third is the inability to reject evil instruction (Pro 19:27)."[75] The wife of your youth is like a loving, tender doe, and the husband should be intoxicated with satisfaction in the pleasures of her body, love, and affection that she gives him.

Why should you be intoxicated, my son, with a strange woman: Stranger: (Heb. *zār*) was applied to those who forsook what was in harmony with the Mosaic Law and so were estranged from God. Thus, in Proverbs, the one morally estranged harlot or prostitute is referred to as a "strange (Heb. *zār*) woman." (Prov. 2:16; 5:17; 7:5.)

---

[73] TANAKH (New Jewish Publication Society Version)

[74] John H Walton, Zondervan Illustrated Bible Backgrounds Commentary (Old Testament): The Minor Prophets, Job, Psalms, Proverbs, Ecclesiastes, Song of Songs, vol. 5 (Grand Rapids, MI: Zondervan, 2009), 476.

[75] Victor P. Hamilton, "2325 שָׁגָה", in Theological Wordbook of the Old Testament, ed. R. Laird Harris, Gleason L. Archer, Jr. and Bruce K. Waltke, electronic ed., 904 (Chicago: Moody Press, 1999).

And embrace the bosom of a foreigner: While a **foreign** (Heb. *nāk·rî*) woman was initially, in the Israelite history, a reference to an immoral woman, who were morally alienated from God and came from outside of Israel; however, in time the term *foreign woman* came to include any prostitute or adulteress. Her smooth words were flattering and seductive. God created man so that he should be exhilarated with his own wife not the breasts of a foreigner, the wife of another mam.

How do we close out this section, by looking at the implications of our day? Why would there be a need for any man or woman for that matter to place themselves in *innocent appearing situations* by flirting in the workplace because the spouse is not there, by a teenager living a different lifestyle while at school, or by spending time alone with someone of the opposite sex? Why be enticed into sexual affection outside of the marriage? The Christian loves to exaggerate their abilities by saying, 'my faith would never allow me to be unfaithful,' or 'the Holy Spirit will protect me from advancements of the stranger,' or simply, 'I would never cheat on my spouse.' These are all *innocent appearing mindsets* of fools. The Bible is full of warnings to all Christians, even those who believe that they are so spiritually strong that they would never stumble. In fact, these warnings are most appropriate for these latter ones, as they are willfully blind and ignorant of their own sinful nature. James writes, "But each one is tempted when he is carried away and enticed by his own desire [or own lust]. Then the desire when it has conceived gives birth to sin, and sin when it is fully grown brings forth death." – James 1:14-15.

Everything Is Openly Exposed to the One Who Examines Us

Proverbs 5:21 Updated American Standard Version (UASV)

²¹ For a man's ways are before the eyes of Jehovah,
   and he examines all his paths.

For a man's ways are before the eyes of Jehovah: Here **ways**: (Heb. *dĕ·rĕk*) is a course of conduct, what is done, the manner in which you conduct yourself on this journey filled with life-choices that you make in this imperfect age of Satan's world. The father is giving the son the way to go by way of wisdom. Proverbs 4:11 tells us that the father has taught the son **the way** (*dĕ·rĕk*) **of wisdom**; the father has led the son in the paths of uprightness. The apostle Peter tells us "the eyes (Gr. *ophthalmos*) of the Lord [the Father] are on the righteous, and his ears are open to their prayer. But the face of the Lord is against those who do evil." (1 Pet 3:12) The Father emphasizes this love, this care, and sensitiveness for all of his servant's welfare. The Psalmist writes, "The eyes of Jehovah are toward the righteous and his ears toward their cry." (Psalm 34:15) How reassuring and heartening it is to know that the Father understands our circumstances and takes notice of our heartfelt supplications!

And he examines all his paths: Here to **examine** (Heb. *pā·lăs*) means that the Father is giving careful thought and consideration, thinking about, pondering, overserving our paths. Paths (Heb. *mă'·gāl*) is figuratively referring to **the ways** (line one) that we conduct ourselves in life as in a well-worn path. This is either conforming to the moral standard of God as we focus on the proper spiritual course of life by observing the indicators (Scriptures) on the path, which leads to life, of which there are few who on it; or, we can follow the paths (ways in line one), which is spacious and leads to destruction, of which there are many who are on it. The Father is aware of our actions even in the darkness. Yes, everything is openly exposed to the One who **examines all of our paths** (ways), for which we will have an accounting one day. Therefore, whether our actions are good or bad, they all are **examined** by God.

We began Proverbs chapter 5, by looking at the consequences of immoral behavior. The reality is that our actions, even our desires that are not immediately dismissed, are "before the eyes of Jehovah." Regardless of how well we might believe that we are hiding inappropriate sexual desires, or worse still acting on those sexual inappropriate desires, it will ruin our relationship with God, as he sees all things. Is some brief immediate gratification worth losing the most precious relationship we can have, with God? Moreover, nothing stays hidden forever, and the wife will eventually discover this dirty secret sinful life.

The Importance of Self-Discipline and Self-Control

Proverbs 5:22-23 Updated American Standard Version (UASV)

22 The errors of the wicked ensnare him,
   and he is held in the cords of his sin.
23 He will die for lack of discipline,
   and because of his great foolishness he will go astray.

The errors of the wicked ensnare him: Error: The Hebrew noun of the Old Testament ('āwōn) and the Greek (*anomia, paranomia*) if the New Testament relates to erring, acting illegally or wrongly. This aspect of sin refers to committing a perverseness, wrongness, lawlessness, law-breaking, which can also include the rejection of the sovereignty of God. It is an act or a feeling that steps over the line of God's moral standard, as something God forbids, or the person ignores carry out (doing) something that God requires, whether it be by one's thoughts, feelings, speech, or actions. It also focuses on the liability or guilt of one's wicked, wrongful act. This error may be deliberate or accidental; either willful deviation of what is right or unknowingly making a mistake. (Lev. 4:13-35; 5:1-6, 14-19; Num. 15:22-29; Ps 19:12-13) Of course, if it is intentional; then, the consequence is far more serious. (Num. 15:30-31) **Error** is in opposition to the truth, and those willfully sinning corrupt the truth, a course that only brings forth flagrant sin. (Isa 5:18-23) We can be hardened by the deceitfulness of sin. – Ex 9:27, 34-35; Heb. 3:13-15.

The Hebrew (*lā·ḵǎḏ*) translated **ensnare** here means, in essence, *to be captured, to be taken over, to be overthrown, to be caught*, the sense *being seized* and *to be taken control of without authority*. The person is *taken control of by force*, which here means the force can come from two places: an outside source or internally. He is taken control of by the force (influence) of the wicked one, or he is taken control of by the force (influence) of his own sinful desires, which overcome his lack of self-disciple, this being the case based on the first line of verse 23.

He will die for lack of discipline: He is taken control of by the force, i.e., **ensnared,** (influenced) by his own sinful desires, which overcome his lack of self-disciple. Self-disciple and self-control (Heb. *mû·sār*) are the moral qualities of a wise person. (Prov. 1:3) A servant of God is obligated to be satisfied with his one wife.

And because of his great foolishness he will go astray: The foolishness (Heb. *'iw·wě·lěṯ*) of the foolish one, who has the trait of acting stupidly or rashly because he is devoid of wisdom or understanding, the Hebrew noun focusing on the evil behaviors which occur in this state. The Hebrew verb (*šā·ḡā(h)*) means to **go astray**, wander, stray, err, to sin either intentionally or unintentionally by being led astray due to the wicked one's influence or one's own lack of self-discipline or self-control.

An unwise person lacks discipline, the ability to control oneself. His life is led by his fleshly desires. His wife no longer captivates this foolish young man, as he is spellbound by his own sinful desires, which lead him to ruination.

BIBLE DIFFICULTIES Proverbs Chapters 5

PROVERBS 5:3 Why is a prostitute called "a strange woman"?

The (*zār*) **strange woman** (2:16) is referring to those who set aside what was in harmony with the Mosaic Law and thus distanced and estrange themselves from God. Therefore, the immoral sensual woman (prostitute) was not necessarily a foreigner. "The strange woman," the prostitute, is described as one "who forsakes the companion of her youth" (2:17), which is referring to the husband of her young womanhood. She has ignored and disregarded the prohibition on adultery that was a part of **the covenant of her God,** the Mosaic Law covenant. — Ex. 20:14; Jeremiah 2:25; 3:13.

CHAPTER 18 Warning Against the Adulteress

INTRODUCTION

Solomon sets out on the difficult task of helping his son (in essence all you people), to see that marriage is a beautiful arrangement, while a life of immorality will only bring pain and difficulty, if not death. The reality is quite simple, if we heed his counsel, we will live. On the other hand, if we ignore his counsel, we will die. While one may get by with a life of immorality and not contract a sexually transmitted disease that contributes to an early death, they will not receive everlasting life, so they are just the walking dead because that is their eventuality.

Receive My Words and Live

Proverbs 7:1-2 Updated American Standard Version (UASV)

7 My son, keep my words
  and treasure up my commandments with you;
² keep my commandments and live;
  keep my teachings[76] as the pupil of your eye;[77]

My son, keep my words: Once again, Solomon opens his writings with a plea to his son, to heed his words and live. Three times in verses 1-2, Solomon uses the imperative verb **keep** (*šā·mǎr*), which is an exhortation or a command for the son to conform their actions to the wise words of their father.

And treasure up my commandments with you: Here **commandment** (*miṣ·wā(h)*) is an authoritative direction or instruction, given as a prescription from the father with the authority or power to the son under his authority or control within the family. – 1 Samuel 13:13; 1 Ki 2:43.

Keep my commandments and live: Only by heeding the father's exhortation to keep his instruction can the son hope to have life and **live** (Heb. *ḥā·yā(h)*).

Keep my teachings as the pupil of your eye: The Hebrew word (*'î·šôn*) **pupil** when used with (*ǎ·yin*) **eye**, it literally means *little man*. (Deut. 32:10) The reference is clearly to the tiny reflected image of yourself that you can see in that black center of another's eye. Similarly, (*bǎṯ*) **daughter** is used at

---

[76] Or *law; instructions*
[77] Lit *little man;* Or *apple of your eye;* I.e., *something precious*

Lamentations 2:18 and literally means "daughter of the eye," a term of endearment. Both expressions are referring to the pupil. The two are combined for emphasis at Psalm 17:8 (*'î·šôn băt-'ă·yin*), which literally means "little man, daughter of the eye." The expression **pupil of your eye** is referring to something precious. In other words, the son needs to keep the laws or teachings of the father as something precious in his eyes.

The importance of this message is to be guarded, to be treasured, and to be kept. The warning here is not just an exhortation it is a command. It is the father, who has been assigned by God to teach God's Word to the children of the family, with the assistance of the wife. Jehovah commanded the Israelite men "And these words that I command you today shall be on your heart. You shall teach them diligently to your children and shall talk of them when you sit in your house, and when you walk by the way, and when you lie down, and when you rise." (Deut. 6:6-7) This is carried over into the New Testament, where Paul stated, "Fathers, do not provoke your children to anger, but bring them up in the discipline and instruction of the Lord." (Eph. 6:4) Yes, the father is charged with regularly, daily instructing his children in the Word of God, to get it down into the heart. The mother is to assist in this task as well, as Solomon spoke of "your mother's teaching," namely, the "law of your mother." – Proverbs 1:8; 6:20

The eye is a very precious organ of sight that is very sensitive to touch. If you have ever experienced even a small speck of dust in your eye, it can be extremely painful, irritating, and cause damage if left in. The cornea is the transparent membrane that covers the pupil and iris of the eye, which needs to be protected and cared for because if for some reason it is damaged or gets diseased, this will result in distorted vision, even blindness. The pupil of the eye is "deeply entrenched in the skull, ramparted with the forehead and cheekbones, defended by the eyebrows, eyelids, and eyelashes, and placed so as to be best protected by the hands."[78] Hence, Solomon with a metaphorical expression uses "the pupil of your eye" in speaking of that, which is to be protected with the greatest concern. The same holds true of the counsel, the commands given here in Proverbs chapter 7.

Taking In the Life Sustaining Knowledge

Proverbs 7:3 Updated American Standard Version (UASV)

³ Bind them on your fingers;
  write them on the tablet of your heart.

---

[78] The Treasury of Scripture Knowledge: Five Hundred Thousand Scripture References and Parallel Passages., Prov. 7:2 (Oak Harbor: Logos Research Systems, Inc., 1995).

Bind them on your fingers: If we recall from Proverbs 3:3, the learner was instructed to "bind them [the teachings] around your neck; write them on the tablet of your heart." The **fingers** (Heb. *ʾeṣ·bāʿ*) of our hands are ever before our eyes, doing the vital work that sustains us. Similarly, the Word of God should have been before our eyes as we grew as a child, or came to God as an adult, taking in the life-sustaining knowledge, acquiring wisdom, which serves as a constant reminder in the way that we should walk. Wisdom if worn by the servant of God as an accessory **like a ring on our finger**, it will make us more attractive to the Creator and to others who see us. It is a witness in and of itself.

Write them on the tablet of your heart: These teachings were/are to be inscribed 'on the tablet of our heart,' to become the very nature of who we are so that we can apply them in our lives with ease. The teachings of God's Word, we are to make them a part of who we are as a person. The biblical lessons learned from Scriptural training or the gaining of Bible knowledge either through personal Bible study or in the Christian congregation are to be a continual reminder and guide us in everything that we do. We are to **write them upon the tablet of our heart**, making them the very part of our nature.

In the ancient world, writing was often done on tablets. While in Mesopotamia writing tablets were normally made of clay, in the Old Testament the term probably refers to wooden boards covered with wax, though the Ten Commandments were written on two stone tablets (Ex. 24:12). The metaphor of the heart as a tablet (not a tablet worn on a cord over the heart, as some would have it) on which one writes the law, of course, points to an internalization of God's commands in one's life, so that not only one's actions but also one's motives are pure (see also Prov. 7:3; Jer. 31:33). The only other place where writing on the heart is specifically mentioned is Jeremiah 17:1, where Judah is said to have written sin on their hearts.[79]

Love Wisdom Instead of an Immoral Woman

Proverbs 7:4 Updated American Standard Version (UASV)

4 Say to wisdom, "You are my sister,"
 and call understanding[80] one who is known,[81]

---

[79] John H Walton, Zondervan Illustrated Bible Backgrounds Commentary (Old Testament) Volume 5: The Minor Prophets, Job, Psalms, Proverbs, Ecclesiastes, Song of Songs, 474-75 (Grand Rapids, MI: Zondervan, 2009).

[80] Or *insight*

[81] I.e. *intimate friend*; that is *to know*, which is often used as a euphemism for secual intercourse

Say to wisdom, "You are my sister,": In the Hebrew Old Testament sister was often used as a term of endearment in reference to a wife or lover. On this John H Walton writes, "The reference to Woman Wisdom as 'sister' must be understood in the context of ancient Near Eastern and biblical love poetry ('my sister, my bride,' Song 4:9), where the 'sister' is actually the beloved. In other words, the father encourages his son to make Woman Wisdom his lover, his wife."[82]

And call understanding one who is known: The Hebrew (Heb. *bî·nā(h)*) term for understanding can also be rendered insight. **Understanding** (Heb. *t^eḇû·nā(h)*) is the ability to see how the parts or aspects of something are connected to one another. One who possesses understanding can see the big picture (the entire matter) and not just the isolated facts. – Prov. 2:5; 9:10; 18:15.

Insight (Heb. *bî·nā(h)*) is the ability to see into a situation. One who possesses insight acts with wisdom, caution, and discretion. Insight is closely related to understanding, but there is a fine distinction between the two terms. Says the *Theological Wordbook of the Old Testament:* "While *bin* [understanding] indicates 'distinguishing between,' [*sa·khal*] relates to an intelligent knowledge of the reason. There is the process of thinking through a complex arrangement of thoughts resulting in a wise dealing and use of good practical common sense. Another end result is the emphasis upon being successful." – Psa. 14:12; Edited by R. L. Harris, 1980, Vol. 2, p. 877

Godly wisdom is having good sense, the ability to make sensible decisions and judgments based on Bible knowledge and your biblically trained conscience. "In Old Testament culture, sister was a term of endearment for a wife or lover (Song 4:9-10, 12; 5:1-2)."[83] Thus, the son is presented with the option of loving two different women: the wife personified as **wisdom** or the **adulteress**. Insight for a person of God specifically, is the ability to see clearly and biblically into the nature of an issue, situation, or matter.

A Naive Young Man Must Choose His Path

Proverbs 7:5 Updated American Standard Version (UASV)

---

[82] John H Walton, *Zondervan Illustrated Bible Backgrounds Commentary (Old Testament): The Minor Prophets, Job, Psalms, Proverbs, Ecclesiastes, Song of Songs*, vol. 5 (Grand Rapids, MI: Zondervan, 2009), 479.

[83] Anders, Max (2005-07-01). Holman Old Testament Commentary - Proverbs (p. 60). B&H Publishing. Kindle Edition. We should love and value wisdom as though she were our sister.

⁵ to keep you from a strange woman,⁸⁴
   from the adulteress with her smooth words.

To keep you from a strange woman: The wise words of the father, his commandment if understood and applied should keep the son from a strange woman or wayward woman. Here the **strange woman** (Heb. *zā·rā(h)*) (2:16; 5:3) is referring to those who set aside what was in harmony with the Mosaic Law and thus distanced and estranged themselves from God. Therefore, the immoral sensual woman (prostitute) was not necessarily a foreigner. "The strange woman," the prostitute, is described as one "who forsakes the companion of her youth" (2:17), which is referring to the husband of her young womanhood. She has ignored and disregarded the prohibition on adultery that was a part of **the covenant of her God**, the Mosaic Law covenant. – Exodus 20:14; Jeremiah 2:25; 3:13.

From the adulteress with her smooth words: The father is now moving into his cautionary account of a naive young son seduced by the wiles of an adulteress woman and his own sinful nature. Her **smooth** (Heb. *ḥā·lāq*) **words**, as you will recall from 5:3, are smoother than oil, they are flattering and seductive, as well as deceitful.

Why is it extremely important that the son develop the teachings of the father (God's Word) and an intimate relationship with wisdom? This will enable the son to dismiss and bypass the seduction of the adulteress. If he chooses to ignore the counsel of his father, her words to him are going to be so smooth and flattering that he will be unable to see the trail leading to her house of death. However, if he chooses to heed his father's counsel, it will especially help him to sidestep the pitfalls of sexual immorality.

A Young Man Lacking Good Sense

Proverbs 7:6-7 Updated American Standard Version (UASV)

⁶ For at the window of my house
   I looked out through my lattice,
⁷ and I saw among the simple,
   I have perceived among the youths,
   a young man in want of heart,⁸⁵

The time of day was just after sunset, the sun had just dropped below the horizon. Solomon was standing in a room of his home, looking out to a street below. The streets are filled with the darkness of the night. He takes notice of a young man heading down the street below.

---

⁸⁴ Or *wayward woman*
⁸⁵ I.e. *lacking good sense*

For at the window of my house: Here the **window** (Heb. ḥǎl·lôn) of his house is not to be confused with the glass window of today but rather it was simply an opening in a wall on a roofed platform along the outside of a house, level with the ground floor, which may have been covered with vines growing over a trellis, meaning that Solomon could look out at the people below but he himself could not be seen by them.

I looked out through my lattice: A **lattice** (Heb. 'ĕš·nāḇ) window is a structure with an air hole in a wall consisting of strips of wood or metal crossed and fastened together covering the hole, in some decorative pattern, which still allowed some to see through it.

And I saw among the simple: Here the Hebrew word (pĕṭî) rendered **simple** is a translation of the same word from 1:4, which is referring to someone who is easily deceived or persuaded because they lack common sense, showing a lack of wisdom and understanding, yet not beyond the capacity to make changes.

I have perceived among the youths: Here youths (*banim*) is simply referring to young men.

A young man in want of heart: This young man facing an adulterous situation is in **want of heart** (lacked heart), as he is inexperienced, lacking good sense and wisdom, lacking good judgment or discernment, so as to avoid the danger that lies ahead.

As the onset of nightfall arrives, the darkness of the night spills into the streets. Solomon catches sight of a young man who is especially in need of protection because he is vulnerable. He is having little knowledge or experience into the situation that he has placed himself. There is little doubt, he knows very well the type of neighborhood he has entered and what goes on there. However, he likely sees the immediate gratification in this one moment of time, not the full ramifications of what seems like nothing more than a good time.

The Young Man Lacks Wisdom and Insight

Proverbs 7:8-9 Updated American Standard Version (UASV)

[8] passing along the street near her corner,
  and he takes the road to her house,
[9] in the twilight, in the evening of the day,
  at the midst[86] of night and darkness.

---

[86] Lit *pupil* (of the eye)

Passing along the street near her corner: We are given suggestive information that the young man has passed this way before or he at least has knowledge of who lies ahead. Solomon gives us this sense partly from his walking in that he says he is passing along the street near the corner, which is suggestive of directions that infers a certain place. When you reference a corner and a street, it suggests directions. The next line will add to this and verse 15 will show us that they knew one another.

And he takes the road to her house: Here the Hebrew verb **taking** (*tsaad*) has the sense "to stride," which means "to step (walk); to march." This too adds to our suggesting that the young man knew where he was going. **Her house** is referring back to the *strange woman* or wayward, adulterous, seductive woman of verse 5.

In the twilight, in the evening of the day: The Hebrew word (*nesheph*) rendered **twilight** has two meanings: *dusk*, the time at the end of the day but just before dark and *dawn*, the time at the end of the night, just before daylight. The context here is obvious right before the darkness of night, dusk.

At the midst of night and darkness: The RSV and the ESV try to deal with what they perceive to be a conflict between the first and second line of verse 9 by rendering the second line of verse 9 as "at the **time** of night and darkness." Here Solomon is building our interest in the adulteress account in that he tells us that as the man walking in the twilight, the night of darkness is upon him. The literal meaning of the Hebrew word rendered **time** (*ishon*) literally means "*the pupil* (of the eye)." It is the black middle or center of the eye, which suggests a *middle time*, that is, the middle of the night. However, there is no real conflict from one line to the next here, as Solomon is simply building the story and, in the poetic, moving from one thought of **twilight** to another thought of **middle of the night**, this is quite normal in Hebrew parallelism.

The young man is in danger, because he lacks wisdom and insight, possibly not fully realizing the end consequences of what part of town he has entered, or maybe he does. Because of Solomon's wisdom, he was able to see the outcome, knowing the young man did not have a chance. Solomon watches intently as the young man nears the strange woman's corner, entering the road to her house. He is deliberately ambiguous as to whether the young man is purposely heading to her house, or simply passing through. It is like he is leaving bread crumbs to the listener or reader of the account, so as to not step on the part of the story that lies ahead.

Temptation In Plain Sight Yet Hidden from the Foolishly Blind

Proverbs 7:10-12 Updated American Standard Version (UASV)

10 And look, a woman comes to meet him,
   dressed as a prostitute,[87] and guarded in heart.[88]
11 She is loud and rebellious;
   her feet do not stay at home;
12 now in the street, now in the square,
   and at every corner she lies in wait.

And look, a woman comes to meet him: The Hebrew here for **woman** is just that an adult female. Of course, this is the same wayward woman that has been a part of the account all along. She and the young man have come to meet in the darkness of night, which now assures of our earlier suspicions that they know each other, and this young man had passed this way before or he at least has knowledge of the wayward woman who was to meet him.

Dressed as a prostitute, and guarded in heart: Well, the language is becoming more plain (clearer) and more obvious. **Guarded in heart** or secret of heart means that she is skilled at being deceitful, very cunning or crafty. The Hebrew term (*natsar*) means that she is evil and causes much damage by her deceptive, secretive, underhanded ways.

She is loud and rebellious: Her becoming **loud** (Heb. *hemmah*) and animated in speech and manner is likely a deflection from her wayward ways. Her being **rebellious** or wayward means that she is stubbornly refusing to change her ways. She was a wayward woman with a spirit of independence, who had no respect in her rebelliousness for God and her husband.

Her feet do not stay at home: This is a poetic way of saying that she does not stay at home. She was constantly roaming the streets looking for new lovers.

Now in the street, now in the square: This **now ... now** is telling us that same as the previous line, she is never home. One moment she is in the street, the next moment she is in the public square (the central part of a city where people meet, and local activities took place), looking for her next lover.

---

87 Or *whore*
88 Or *secret of heart*; I.e. *a cunning heart*

And at every corner she lies in wait: The expression **lies in wait** is a military saying, which refers to setting an ambush so as to capture one's prey, bringing them much harm.

The young man is now introduced to the strange woman and her character. We get the sense immediately that her manner is alluring, as she is dressed like a prostitute. While her close gives everything away, the text says she is guarded in heart (cunning of heart), meaning that she has a hidden agenda, secretive, crafty and deceitful. She moves about loudly and stubbornly, looking for the next lover, in the street, in the public square, lying-in-wait at every street corner for her prey, seeking someone just like this young man. This wayward woman's loud seductive behavior in the public square evidences her immodesty.

Steps That Lead to Immorality

Proverbs 7:13 Updated American Standard Version (UASV)

[13] She seizes him and kisses him,
    and with bold face she says to him,[89]

She seizes him and kisses him: The Hebrew for **seizes** is simply that she took hold of him, while the Hebrew for **kissing** (*nashaq*) him is not as one does in greeting another in all other occurrences, but rather here and Song of Solomon 1:2 and 8:1, it has a sexual significance.

And with bold face she says to him: This literally says that *She makes bold her face and says*, while others say it is literally *she makes her face strong and says*. In essence, what is meant by her putting on a bold or strong face is that she has no shame, nor does she have any regret for her adulterous, temptress behavior.

We must understand that there are stages to every temptation. **First,** it enters the mind, meaning we can dismiss it and rationalize the repercussions of such thinking; this is not the difficult stage. **Second,** there is the entertaining and cultivating the thought(s), which has the ability to affect us emotionally, mentally and physically. When this goes on too long, it can become very difficult to turn back. **Third,** there is the initial commitment, like the young man choosing the street to go down where he knows the prostitute will be. He can turn back still, but the train of emotions is moving, and it is far more difficult to bring the sensations to a halt. **Fourth,** there is the entering the lion's den, where he is actively involved, as the prey of his own sinful nature. At this point, she is touching him, kissing him with her smooth lips, the scent of her perfume, so every sensation has taken hold of him. The possibility of turning back is near

---

[89] Lit *She makes bold her face and says*

impossible. Regardless of the inappropriate desire, there are stages that make it even more difficult to turn back.

Seeing Empty Deceptive Words for What They Are

Proverbs 7:14 Updated American Standard Version (UASV)

[14] "I had to offer peace offerings,
and today I have paid my vows;

I had to offer peace offerings: Here statement of offering the **peace offering** is her way of hinting that she did not lack spirituality. The peace offerings set forth in Leviticus 7:11–17; 19:5-6; 22:21; Numbers 15:8-10 consisted of meat, flour, oil, and wine. Therefore, she was deceptively inferring that there was much to eat and drink at her house and that the **young man in want of heart** (6:7) was certain to have a good time. She knew that he is inexperienced, lacking good sense and wisdom, lacking good judgment or discernment, so he would not see the danger in her seductive ways or her words.

And today I have paid my vows: The vow offering, which is voluntary, is associated with the making of a vow (promises) to God or to perform some act, to make some offering, enter into some action of helping or doing work, or to refrain from certain things not unlawful in themselves until such time as he had been able to attain a certain goal, with the help of God. According to Leviticus 7:16, "if the sacrifice of his offering is a **vow** offering or a freewill offering, it shall be eaten on the day that he offers his sacrifice, and on the next day what remains of it shall be eaten." This is characteristic of just how a wrongly motivated person can be guided into immorality.

The wayward woman's words are carefully chosen, and suggestive to the Israelite mind. This might seem very strange coming from the voice of a prostitute, **(1)** maybe suggesting that she is a devout woman, who is ceremonially clean. **(2)** It is suggestive of her cleanness after her menstruation cycle. **(3)** Rather she could be simply urging him to join her in a meal of the meat and wine left over from her peace offering, as the one offering the sacrifices get to take part of the offering home. (Lev. 19:5, 6; 22:21; Num. 15:8-10) Regardless, she has touched this young man's senses, taking him to a whole other level of danger, with her smooth voice, and her suggestive comments. Old Testament Bible scholar, John Walton says,

It is best to understand the offerings in the light of Leviticus 3 and 7:11–21. The fellowship offering emphasizes communion between the worshiper and God as well as with fellow worshipers. The meat must be eaten on the same day as the sacrifice. Thus, the woman is trying to entice the man not only with her body but with a delicious meal. But her acts just accentuate the sinfulness of her acts, adding the misuse of holy things (the sacrifice) to adultery.[90]

Often, as we spoke of in verse 13, there are stages that we can identify that lead to immorality. Each stage that we take makes it increasingly difficult for us to turn back.

Flattering Words

Proverbs 7:15 Updated American Standard Version (UASV)

[15] So I have come out to meet you,
to seek your face, and I have found you.

So I have come out to meet you: You will recall from 7:5, the father stated: "to keep you from a strange woman, from the adulteress with her smooth words." Now we see the beginning of her smooth words in that she begins her flattery of inferring that it is him alone that she seeks, no other.

To seek your face, and I have found you: Here again, the literal **seek your face**, is a wayward woman with flattering words, as it means "to seek you eagerly," as she eagerly seeks him alone, to know him. The sense of **found you** is more than a mere encountering him but rather a searching out for him alone. These words suggest even more that they have met before and her excited words for him may very well be believable to him.

When lust has the better of this young man, his thinking ability is not registering her unbelievable, misleading words. Unquestionably, she did not come out of her house, to meet this young man specifically, as if he was special to her, to seek his face, it is a sham. Only a foolish person, moved by intense emotions, would believe such words.

Seducing the Senses

Proverbs 7:16-17 Updated American Standard Version (UASV)

[16] I have spread my couch with coverings,
colored linens from Egyptian linen;
[17] I have sprinkled[91] my bed with myrrh,
aloes, and cinnamon.

---

[90] John H Walton, Zondervan Illustrated Bible Backgrounds Commentary (Old Testament) Volume 5: The Minor Prophets, Job, Psalms, Proverbs, Ecclesiastes, Song of Songs, 479 (Grand Rapids, MI: Zondervan, 2009).
[91] I.e. *perfumed*

I have spread my couch with coverings: The Hebrew verb (*rabad*) is found only here on the Hebrew Old Testament, which means to **spread over** or **cover**. This seductress is clearly a woman of great wealth, as the items from verses 16 and 17 are all exported goods. The Hebrew word rendered **couch** (*eres*) can refer to a wooden pallet on the floor in the home the common people. However, here the term **couch** shows evidence of her wealth when it is considered with the rest of the items, which is used for both resting and sleeping and is found only in the homes of wealthy people.

Colored linens from Egyptian linen: There is an extra cost in adding color in the manufacturing of these linens, for it is an additional step in the process. Here the temptress is flaunting her wealth and uses the bright colors in an attempt at seducing this man into her bedchamber.

I have sprinkled my bed with myrrh: Here the Hebrew verb (*nuph*) rendered **sprinkled** means that she perfumed her bed. Myrrh is a fragrant gum resin obtained from various thorny shrubs or small trees and is one of the ingredients for the holy anointing oil. (Ex. 30:23-25) It was highly valued for its fragrance. it was used to scent garments, beds, and other items. (See Ps 45:8; Prov. 7:17; Song of Solomon 3:6-7) It was often used with other spices like those below to cause sexual excitement.

aloes, and cinnamon: These spices, including the myrrh, were also used for lovemaking and believed to possess a stimulant that causes sexual desires. (See Song of Solomon 4:6) The seductress is describing these spices in order to entice the young man into having sexual relations with her. The adulteress uses these pleasant foreign sweet-smelling fragrances to transform her bedchamber into a striking colorful eye-catching, perfumed, desirable trap.

She offers the young man more visuals, giving him images to motivate him to enter her home. Her revealing clothing has moved this young man along with the sensual sound of her pleasing words, in addition to the touch of her embrace, as well as the taste of her smooth lips, on top of the scent of her perfume. This is a train wreck just waiting to happen. It is now all too clear to the young man that he is going into her home for a sexual experience. In the imperfect human condition, our senses can be used against us by Satan's world that caters to the flesh. Wrong desires are gratifying to us in this condition. Just as the scent of a meal can contribute to a physical (salivating and hunger pains), mental (thinking on) and emotional reaction (desiring) from us; so too a young man can lose his self-control in a sexual frenzy and go after a prostitute.

Reviewing once more, this young man did not reach this sexual frenzy stage all at once; it came in the stages that we spoke of earlier. Now, let us talk about the initial steps involved **(1)** entertaining the thinking that moved him to **(2)** walking on her street at night, **(3)** permitting her to kiss him, and **(4)** paying attention to her immoral offers. As he entered each of these steps, it became far more difficult to turn back. He should have dismissed the thinking at step one (James 1:14-15), before he ever found himself on her street. Even then, once he was walking down her street, he needed to stop, and turn back. – Galatians 5:22-23.

The Seductive Invitation

Proverbs 7:18 Updated American Standard Version (UASV)

¹⁸ Come, let us drink our fill of love until morning;
  let us delight ourselves with love.

Come, let us drink our fill of love until morning: Here drink our fill means to take our fill or to fully experience our lovemaking as much as possible. The Hebrew noun rendered **love** (*dod*) is in the plural form here and in the second line are used in the Old Testament only in a sexual sense and refer to sexual intercourse between two people. The context here is an immoral sexual contact. **Until morning** has the sense of all night long.

Let us delight ourselves with love: The Hebrew rendered **delight** (*alas*) means to enjoy, to take pleasure in each other with lovemaking all night.

The strange woman ends her offer with a night filled with lovemaking. How many young ones have fallen to these types of exploits today? When someone is trying to entice you into sexual misconduct, it is not loving within the lovemaking, but rather it is selfish lust. Would a man or a woman who truly loves someone pressure them into violating their Christian values?

My Husband Is Gone!

Proverbs 7:19-20 Updated American Standard Version (UASV)

¹⁹ Because the man[92] is not in his house;
  he has gone on the road far off;[93]
²⁰ he took a bag of silver[94] in his hand;
  at full moon he will come home."

Because the man is not in his house: This can be rendered "my husband is not at home." All along the wayward woman has been trying to seduce this young man with her body language and her choice of the right words.

---

[92] Or *my husband is not at home*
[93] I.e. *a long journey*
[94] Or *money*

124

So, her choice of saying **the man** in place of "my man" is just her way of distancing herself from the concept of her having a husband in her continued efforts to encourage the young man. When translations avoid the literal translation because it sounds wooden or peculiar; they, also deprive the reader of protentional meaning.

He has gone on the road far off: The literal rendering **on the road far off** means *a long journey.* This is her clearly trying to relieve the young man of any fear of their being caught by an enraged husband.

He took a bag of silver in his hand: This would likely have not been minted coins, namely, manufactured coins of specified values using a kind of stamping, but rather he likely took bulk silver, which would have to have been weighed, signaling that the man took lots of money for purchasing purposes, inferring that he will be away for a long time.

At full moon he will come home: Yet, another inference, **full moon** (*kese* or *keseh*), suggesting that the man (her husband) was going to be away for a long time. She is basically saying they, "he will not be back until the first of the month." Remember, verse 9 of chapter 7 said, "at the midst of night and darkness," which can refer to the new moon, some two weeks before the full moon. The **full moon** is the brightest phase of the **moon in the** lunar month while the **new moon** is the darkest.

Maybe she sees a fear in the young man's heart, the only thing causing him pause, so she moves to remove his concerns of being caught, telling him that her husband is off "on a long journey," and will not be back for many days, per the reference to taking a big bag of money with him. Therefore, he needs not fear any consequences for this night of endless pleasure will bring.

Seductive Words

Proverbs 7:21 Updated American Standard Version (UASV)

²¹ She   persuades   him   with   much   seductive   words; with her smooth lips she compels him.

She persuades him with much seductive words: The Hebrew word for **persuade** (*natah*) means to bend or turn aside, namely, to cause someone to wander from a proper belief or behavior, conduct, course of action. The wayward woman is persuading this young man to turn aside from his values by her seductive words to engage in an adulterous immoral behavior. Here the Hebrew word (*leqach*) for **seductive words** is referring to persuasive words. Words that have the power to change one's mind through persuasion, which in turn can change one's feeling and behavior as well. *Leqach*, the art of persuasion, can be used for good or bad. In Proverbs 1:5

it is used for learning and in 4:2, it is used for good teaching, and here in 7:21 it is being used for an alluring, tempting, seducing, enticing, encouraging the adulterous immoral behavior.

With her smooth lips she compels him: Her **smooth** (Heb. *ḥā·lāq*) **words** of 7:5, as you will also recall from 5:3, are **smoother than oil**, they are flattering and seductive, as well as deceitful, are now being referred to as **smooth lips** (*cheleq*), which is a figure of speech used to stand for what she is saying. This is excessive insincere flattery. This is a manner of speaking that contains content that is designed to persuade, which in this context, it is sexually suggestive or rather **seductive words**. The Hebrew word (*nadach*) means that she is using forceful pressure to entice, so as to turn the young man way from what is right.

How gifted she is at enticing, charming, mesmerizing this young man. He has been caught in her seductive words, her smooth words have finally gotten her the results she so desired. The idea of being loved no doubt sounded very good to him. Yet, in reality, the prostitute has misled him by the abundance of her persuasive seductive words. No, she had no actual love for this young man; but rather he was purely a customer. She exploited him to her own selfish desires.

Suddenly Ensnared

Proverbs 7:22-23 Updated American Standard Version (UASV)

22 Suddenly he goes after her,
  as an ox goes to the slaughter,
like a fool to be punished in the fetters
23 till an arrow pierces its liver;
as a bird rushes into a snare;
  he does not know that it will cost him his soul.

Suddenly he goes after her: Here **suddenly** (Heb. *pithom*) might suggest that the young man was hesitant until the wayward woman's seductive words in verse 20-21.

As an ox goes to the slaughter: An **ox** is an adult, castrated male cattle. Slaughter is when animals are killed for food. Here the simile here is that the animal is oblivious (unaware or ignorant) to the idea that he is about to be killed and eaten. This is true of the young man as well, who is oblivious to the idea of the pain and suffering of the consequences that are coming.

Like a fool to be punished in the fetters: This young man has been caught by the seductive, deceptive words of this wayward woman and he will be paying the consequences, as there is no escaping them.

Till an arrow pierces its liver: Syphilis is a serious sexually transmitted disease caused by the spirally twisted bacterium Treponema pallidum that affects many body organs (liver) and parts, including the genitals, brain, skin, and nervous tissue. Gonorrhea is a sexually transmitted bacterial disease that causes inflammation of the liver. The young man has been and is so naïve to the dangers of the trap that has been set before him.

As a bird rushes into a snare: Here the Hebrew word rendered **rush** (*mahir*) means that this impetuous, hurried, rash young man with no wisdom or sense is about to suddenly enter into the trap that has been laid before him. He is unaware or ignorant to the trap that lies before him and in but a single moment of time, it is too late to escape or go back, and his life is forever altered, if not destroyed.

He does not know that it will cost him his soul: This means that "it will cost him his life." This statement is open-ended as there is no specific way mentioned as to how the young man is going to lose his life. The only possible sense of how is found back in Proverbs 2:16-19.

The young man's breaking point has been reached, as he dismisses and insightful counsel of his father, suddenly he goes after her "like an ox to a slaughter." Just as the similes[95] used by Solomon, this young man does not realize that his passionate frenzy is going to cost him his life. Hence, he hurries into a perilous situation of death like a bird into a trap! "The figure of an arrow piercing the liver (an implied comparison) may refer to the pangs of a guilty conscience that the guilty must reap along with the spiritual and physical ruin that follows."[96]

The Father's Final Warning Against a Strange Woman

Proverbs 7:24-25 Updated American Standard Version (UASV)

24 And now, O sons, listen to me,
   and be attentive to the words of my mouth.
25 Let not your heart turn aside to her ways;
   do not stray into her paths.

And now, O sons, listen to me: Here **and** is being used to close out the counsel, which is why it is rendered **and now**. The father, using a term of endearment, **O sons**, before giving his final commands, pleading for his

---

[95] A simile is a figurative language drawing a comparison: a figure of speech that draws a comparison between two different things, especially a phrase containing the word "like" or "as," e.g. "as white as a sheet." Marilyn turned as white as a sheet when the police officer told her that her son had been in a car wreck. Did something scare you? You are white as a sheet!
[96] Biblical Studies Press, The NET Bible First Edition Notes, Pr 7:23 (Biblical Studies Press, 2006).

sons to **listen** (Heb. *shama*), that is pay attention and obey, never departing from his words.

And be attentive to the words of my mouth: The Hebrew verb (*qā·šaḇ*) **be attentive** means listening and paying close attention, giving heed (i.e., obeying), accepting the instruction as being true and responding to it favorably. The figurative expression **words of my mouth** mean pay attention to what I say, pay attention to what I have taught you, pay attention to my instructions, my commandments.

Let not your heart turn aside to her ways: The Hebrew (*satah*) for **turn away** means that the young man is to turn away from the way or the path of this strange (i.e., wayward) woman that was referred to in 7:5, with this figurative expression, also meaning a change in behavior.

Do not stray into her paths: The Hebrew verb rendered **stray** (*taah*) means that this young man is not to wander from the moral beliefs and values that the father has instilled in him into a course of action that would lead him down her immoral path. Both of these commands are given to help the son to remove himself from this temptation before it has begun to lead him astray, so as to protect his figurative heart, namely his inner person, the seat of motivation. The young man has ignored his morally trained conscience at every stage, from entering the street where he knows that wayward woman will be to meet up with her where her scent can impact him, her words can move him, and her touch can conquer him.

Looking at the Christian today, he has to be able to get control over his thinking. The same young man today can end up on the wrong street, because of entertaining immoral thoughts that enter the mind. As soon as the thought enters his mind, if the Christian conscience is trained, he should dismiss it outright, and then internally rationalize just why that thinking is wrong. If he does not commit himself to this, he will fail by progressing even further toward the actions of viewing porn, masturbation, fornication, or adultery.

No true Christian should follow the literal steps of this man, but what about his thoughts. Could a person mentally begin 'going down the street to her house by dwelling on immoral thoughts? Right then, he needs to put on the brakes! Failing to do so may result in mentally progressing to further steps such as masturbation or eventual sexual immorality.

The Apostle Paul told the Galatians, "Now those who belong to Christ Jesus have crucified the flesh with its passions and desires." (Gal. 5:24) This crucifixion refers Christ in his death and resurrection, and that 'we longer live, but Christ lives in us. The life we now live in the body, we live by faith in the Son of God, who loved us and gave Himself for us.' (Gal. 2:20) This does not mean that we no longer have the thinking and desires that lead to sin. It means that our old personalities are no more, and we are now new people, having the ability to gain control over our thinking. – Romans 6:10-12.

Additionally, as an imperfect people, we need to be vigilant about dismissing any inappropriate thinking that enters our minds, before we begin to entertain and cultivate them. If one is watching a movie or television program, and they begin to have improper thoughts that can lead to sexual desires, they need to change the channel if at home, or get up and walk out of the theater. The Christian mind has to be very cautious as to what the mind takes in, especially in the age of computers, internet, iPads, and smartphones. In addition, all Christians need to be Christlike in their conversations with others, especially non-Christians, and the opposite sex. – Matthew 5:28-30; Colossians 3:5.

For those who struggle in this area, more proactive measures are needed. Once an improper thought has been dismissed, he needs to speak to himself, rationalizing why it is wrong, and what this type of thinking can do to spiritually wreck a Christian life. If he is in bed and an improper thought has entered his mind, he needs to get up and do just that, pray thereafter, and have a Bible handy to read from, before going back to bed. The prayer needs to be ardent, this cannot be lip service.

You Cannot Escape the Cruel, Vicious, Brutal, Ruthless Violence that Leads to Your Fatality

Proverbs 7:26-27 Updated American Standard Version (UASV)

²⁶ For many are the fatally wounded[97] she has made fall,[98]
 and all her slain are a mighty throng.
²⁷ Her house is the way to Sheol,
 descending to the chambers of death.

For many are the fatally wounded she has made fall: Here is the Hebrew noun (*chalal*) is literally rendered **fatally wounded** but elsewhere it is rendered **victim** (ESV) or **slain** (LEB). The sense of this line is that this immoral wayward woman has mortally wounded and brought death to many men.

And all her slain are a mighty army: Solomon is trying to stress the danger by using military language to describe the fatal results of interacting with this wayward woman. **Fatally wounded** can refer to **casualties** and the slain (Heb. *harag*) here are a **mighty throng** (*atsumim*) and can be seen as

---

[97] Or *the victims*
[98] Or *laid low* or *cast down*

a **mighty army**. The verb for **slain** can mean with cruel, vicious, brutal, ruthless violence.

Her house is the way to Sheol: Here **her house** is not simply the building or home that she lives in but rather, it has the sense of what it is that is going on in her house as the focus. (see 2:18 and 5:5. Compare also 9:18) Here **Sheol**: (Heb. *sheol*) occurs sixty-six times in the UASV. The Greek Septuagint renders Sheol as Hades. It has the underlying meaning of a place of the dead, where they are conscious of nothing, awaiting a resurrection, for both the righteous and the unrighteous. (Gen. 37:35; Psa. 16:10; Ac 2:31; John 5:28-29; Acts 24:15) It corresponds to "Hades" in the NT. It does not involve torment and punishment.

Descending to the chambers of death: The Hebrew verb (*yarad*) rendered descending is to move downward or lower with an ominous sense. **Chambers of death** is an expression that is similar to, equivalent to **Sheol**, and is similar to Proverbs 2:18 and 5:5. The Hebrew (*cheder*) **Chambers** is a rendering for a word meaning *rooms* that are located in the inner part of a house or building. Here **Sheol** is seen as a house that has many rooms.

The beauty and seductive power of this strange woman are quite deceptive because she has slain many that have entered her house. To naively believe that you can somehow escape the cruel, vicious, brutal, ruthless violence that leads to your fatality, while a throng of others has not is simply foolish. Some temptations are so consuming that the best recourse, is to stay as far removed as one can. The terminology of verse 26 is military in nature. Thus, young one needs to see the world of humankind that is alienated from God, his own weaknesses and leanings, in addition to Satan, as a war zone. Therefore, he needs to be ever vigilant to his environment.

CHAPTER 19 The Pornography Trap

A 50-year-old married physician views Internet pornography for hours at home, masturbating five to seven times a day, then begins surfing porn sites at the office and risks destroying his career.

A woman spends four to six hours a day in Internet chat rooms and having cybersex, and eventually starts arranging to meet online strangers for casual sex in the real world.

A man spends many hours a day downloading porn, filling multiple hard drives, and devotes a separate computer just to pornography.

A married couple views pornographic movies together as part of their loving relationship, but the husband starts spending more time watching and less time with his wife, who feels left behind and rejected.

These scenarios are real-life examples of pornography addiction, a compulsive behavior that falls within the category of sex addiction.[99]

Pornography addiction or problematic pornography use is a behavioral addiction characterized by compulsive, repeated use of pornographic material until it causes serious negative consequences to one's physical, mental, social, and/or financial well-being. Addiction to Internet pornography is a form of cybersex addiction.

Symptoms and Diagnosis

Diagnostic criteria do not exist for pornography addiction or problematic pornography viewing. A study on problematic Internet pornography viewing used the criteria of viewing Internet pornography more than three times a week during some weeks, and viewing causing difficulty in general life functioning.

In 1990 Aviel Goodman proposed a general definition of all types of addictions in order to extend the specific disorders included in the DSM-III-R. While not explicitly in the context of pornography, Goodman explains his criteria for addiction as a "process whereby a behavior, that can function both to produce pain and to provide escape from internal discomfort, [and] is employed in a pattern characterized by (1) failure to control the behavior

---

[99]   http://www.sfgate.com/health/article/Porn-addiction-destroys-relationships-lives-3272230.php

(powerlessness) and (2) continuation of the behavior despite significant negative consequences (unmanageability)."[100]

According to the San Francisco Chronicle, "If people want to escape feelings of low self-esteem, shame, isolation or the pressures of life, work or relationships, pornography is a place to get lost and feel wanted, imagining the perfect partners who always desires them - and whom they can always satisfy."[101] The Chronicle goes on to say that the risk of job loss and spousal loss is very high with those who are truly addicted to pornography.

Dr. Brown further says, "All too often, sexual addicts risk losing important relationships, being plagued with diseases, and place their jobs and careers on the line. For the addict, it is less about the desire and more about fulfilling a compulsive need."

Prevalence

Though no studies have been conducted on prevalence of pornography addiction, research on Internet addiction disorder indicates rates may range from 1.5 to 8.2% in Europeans and Americans.[102] Internet pornography users are included in Internet users, and Internet pornography has been shown to be the Internet activity most likely to lead to compulsive disorders.[103] A study found that 17% of people who viewed pornography on the Internet met criteria for problematic sexual compulsivity.[104] A survey found that 20–60% of a sample of college-age males who use pornography found it to be problematic.[105]

Status as Addiction

In 2011, the American Society of Addiction Medicine published a definition of addiction that for the first time stated that addiction includes

---

[100] Goodman, Aviel (1990). "Addiction: Definition and implications". Addiction 85 (11): 1403–8.

[101] http://www.sfgate.com/health/article/Porn-addiction-destroys-relationships-lives-3272230.php#ixzz2N3ZSi4o7

[102] Weinstein, A.; Lejoyeux, M. (2010). "Internet Addiction or Excessive Internet Use". The American Journal of Drug and Alcohol Abuse 36 (5): 277–283.

[103] Meerkerk, G. J.; Eijnden, R. J. J. M. V. D.; Garretsen, H. F. L. (2006). "Predicting Compulsive Internet Use: It's All about Sex!". CyberPsychology & Behavior 9 (1): 95–103.

[104] Cooper, A., Delmonico, D. L., & Burg, R. (2000). Cybersex user, abusers, and compulsives. Sexual Addiction and Compulsivity, 7, 5–29.

[105] Twohig, M. P.; Crosby, J. M.; Cox, J. M. (2009). "Viewing Internet Pornography: For Whom is it Problematic, How, and Why?". Sexual Addiction & Compulsivity 16 (4): 253.

pathological pursuit of all kinds of external rewards and not just substance dependence.

The status of pornography addiction as an addictive disorder, rather than simply a compulsivity, is supported by a growing body of evidence but is still contested by some neuroscientists. The current Diagnostic and Statistical Manual of Mental Disorders (DSM-V) includes a new section for behavioral addictions but includes only one disorder: pathological gambling. Other behavioral addictions were included in "Conditions for further study". A 2011 paper by Donald Hilton and Clark Watts argued that studies demonstrating the effect of sexual experiences on neuroplasticity indicate the existence of process addiction, and specifically focused on pornography addiction as an area requiring further study. In a letter to the editor, Rory Reid, Bruce Carpenter, and Timothy Fong responded by arguing that the studies on neuroplasticity used correlational data, and thus could not be used to establish causation. In a commentary included with the letter to the editor, Hilton and Watts pointed to research connecting a marker of addiction, to sexual experience, and claimed that researchers who reject the research they cite are biased against research which connects neuromodulation to behavioral addictions.

Online Pornography

Psychologists who see pornography as addictive may consider online, often Internet pornography more addictive than ordinary pornography because of its wide availability, explicit nature, and the privacy that online viewing offers. Some claim that addicts regularly spend extended periods of time searching the Internet for new or increasingly hardcore pornography.[106]

Some clinicians and support organizations recommend the voluntary use of Internet content-control software, Internet monitoring, or both, to manage online pornography use.

Sex researcher Alvin Cooper and colleagues suggested several reasons for using filters as a therapeutic measure, including curbing accessibility that facilitates problematic behavior and encouraging clients to develop coping and relapse prevention strategies. Cognitive therapist Mary Anne Layden suggested that filters may be useful in maintaining environmental control. Internet behavior researcher David Delmonico noted that, despite their limitations, filters may serve as a "frontline of protection."[107]

---

[106] Downs, Martin F.; Louise Chang, MD (reviewer) (August 30, 2005). "Is Pornography Addictive? Psychologists debate whether people can have an addiction to pornography."
[107] Delmonico, David L. (1997). "Cybersex: High tech sex addiction". Sexual Addiction & Compulsivity 4 (2): 159.

Treatment

Cognitive-behavioral therapy has been suggested as a possible effective treatment for pornography addiction based on its success with Internet addicts though no clinical trials have been performed to assess effectiveness among pornography addicts as of 2012. Acceptance and commitment therapy has also been shown to be a potentially effective treatment for problematic Internet pornography viewing.[108]

Damage to Us Spiritually

Colossians 3:5 Updated American Standard Version (USV)

[5] Deaden, therefore, your members on the earth: sexual immorality,[109] uncleanness, passion, evil desire, and greediness, which is idolatry

> In telling believers to **put to death** certain behaviors, Paul is calling for complete extermination, not careful regulation. What must go? Paul gives us an "outside in" perspective. He starts with external actions and then moves to the internal drives which cause the conduct. In his "vice lists" Paul mentions three categories of behavior: (1) perverted passions, (2) hot tempers, (3) sharp tongues.

> First on the list is **sexual immorality** (*porneia*), a broad, general term for all kinds of illicit sexual behavior. God created sex to be enjoyed by one woman and one man in the confines of marriage. Any sexual activity that does not fit that definition is not to be part of a believer's life. The perverted passion list continues with mention of **impurity**. This reminds us that immorality is "unclean" or dirty and incompatible with the purity of our Savior. Believers are not to be slaves of their **lust** or **evil desires**.[110]

Pornography can end loving relationships. The apostle Peter said, "Husbands, live with your wives in an understanding way, **showing honor** to the woman." If we are looking at images of naked women, or even sensually dressed women, with lustful intent in our heart, how is this

---

[108] http://en.wikipedia.org/wiki/Pornography_addiction

[109] **Sexual Immorality:** (Heb. *zanah*; Gr. *porneia*) A general term for immoral sexual acts of any kind: such as adultery, prostitution, sexual relations between people not married to each other, homosexuality, and bestiality. – Num. 25:1; Deut. 22:21; Matt. 5:32; 1 Cor. 5:1.

[110] Max Anders, vol. 8, Kendell H. Easley, vol. 12, Galatians, Ephesians, Philippians, Colossians, Holman New Testament Commentary, 329 (Nashville, TN: Broadman & Holman Publishers, 1998).

showing honor to our wives? When she discovers such material, is she not going to be devastatingly hurt, feel betrayed, and feel as though she is not enough?

Matthew 5:27-28 Updated American Standard Version (UASV)

27 "You have heard that it was said, 'You shall not commit adultery;'[111] 28 but I say to you that everyone who looks at a woman with lust[112] for her has already committed adultery with her in his heart.

Exodus 20:14, "You shall not commit adultery," which means that we need to value the sanctity of marriage, to remain faithful at times of temptation.

In verse 28 of Matthew chapter 5, you will notice the phrase **"lustful intent,"** keying in on the word "intent." This is not a man walking along who catches sight of a beautiful woman and has an indecent thought, which he then dismisses. It is not even a man in the same situation that has an indecent thought, who goes on to entertain and cultivate that thought. No, this is a man that is staring, gazing at a woman with the intent of lusting, and is looking at the woman, with the intention of peaking her interest and desire, to get her to lust.

Do Not Desire the Immoral Woman's Beauty

Proverbs 6:25-26 Updated American Standard Version (UASV)

25 Do not desire her beauty in your heart,
    and do not let her capture you with her eyelashes;[113]
26 for because of a prostitute, a man is reduced to a loaf of bread,
    but a wife of another man hunts down a precious soul.[114]

Do not desire her beauty in your heart: Here (Heb. *ḥā·mǎḏ*) **desire** is being used in the bad sense in that the young man is being warned against strongly wanting, lusting after, coveting the beauty of another man's wife.

And do not let her capture you with her eyelashes: Here (Heb. *lā·qǎḥ*) **capture** is referring to the young man being seduced or being led astray by the alluring eyes of another man's wife. The Hebrew (*ǎp̄·ʾǎp·pǎ·yim*) is rendered **eyelashes** here but is literally "eyelids," which

---

[111] Ex. 20:14; Deut. 5:17

[112] ἐπιθυμία [*epithumia*] is a strong desire to have what belongs to another, as well as becoming involved in anything that is morally wrong, i.e., coveting, lusting, evil desires, and the like.

[113] I.e. *alluring eyes*

[114] I.e. life

is referring to how a woman uses her alluring eyes to attract the attention of men.

For because of a prostitute, a man is reduced to a loaf of bread: A prostitute is a person, in particular, a woman, who engages in sexual activity for payment. It seems that Solomon is saying that an adulterous wife being referred to as a prostitute may cost as much as a loaf of bread.

But a wife of another man hunts down a precious soul: The adulteress wife endangers the "precious soul," or life, of her adulterous partner. The Hebrew (ṣûḏ) **hunts down** is referring to the husband of the adulteress doing after the adulterous young man, who had sexual relations with his wife, intending to cause him bodily harm or kill him.

Exodus 20:14, "You shall not commit adultery," which means that we need to value the sanctity of marriage, to remain faithful at times of temptation. At Matthew 5:28 Jesus states, "But I say to you that everyone who looks at a woman with lustful intent has already committed adultery with her in his heart." (ESV) Jesus identified the preliminaries, which was a sin in and of itself, that lead up to the sinful act of adultery, as "lustful intent." Focus on the word "intent." This is not a man walking along who catches sight of a beautiful woman and has an indecent thought, which he then dismisses (that is not lusting). It is not even a man in the same situation that has an indecent thought, who goes on to entertain and cultivate that thought (this is lusting and is a sin). No, this is a man that is staring, gazing at a woman with the intent of lusting, and is looking at the woman, with the intention of peaking her interest and desire, to get her to lust.

Verse 25 of chapter 26 in Proverbs warns the son against just that, do not get "lustful intent" in your heart because of her beauty. Yes, even when the evil woman is seeking to flame such desires. Aside from the fact that it violates God's Law, for mere moments of immediate gratification at a very inexpensive price, you are risking your life on a wife, who has a husband that will take your precious life.

James 1:14-15 Updated American Standard Version (UASV)

[14] But each one is tempted when he is carried away and enticed by his own desire.[115] [15] Then the desire when it has conceived gives birth to sin, and sin when it is fully grown brings forth death.

> James states **but each one is tempted**, which signifies that temptation is on an individual basis. The temptation is not another individual's problem but is an individual choice that one gives into or rejects. James also writes one is tempted when he is **carried away and**

---

[115] Or "own *lust*"

enticed by his desire, which exposes that the problem of temptation lies not with God, but rather it is in oneself. James says that temptation is always directed at the desire of one's heart. Therefore, God is not the one who is causing the temptation, but the temptation comes through the enticement of one's lust within his heart.

The Greek word James uses here for enticed is *deleazo*, which means to "*lure as bait*." (Vine 1996, 203) James tells us in the passage that the underlying motivation for all temptation is selfish desire, that all temptations spring from man's desire to satisfy his own flesh and personal forbidden desires. This means the temptation that Satan offers to people always deals with that which is pleasurable to man and appeals to his desires. This is not to say that human desires in and of itself are wrong. Moreover, human pleasure is not bad in and of itself. Satan has corrupted the desires of the flesh, which was perfectly natural before the sin of Adam. For example, there was a natural desire for a physical relationship between man and woman. After the fall, Paul tells us that it has become a standard practice "For their women [to] exchange natural relations for those that are contrary to nature," i.e., homosexuality. (Rom. 1:26) Once the lust is manifested in the heart then the more it lingers there without being dealt with then it will begin to carry away the individual with the enticement of what that fulfilled lust can bring.

Temptation always begins with an enticement towards one's lust or an unwarranted desire. If not cast down, one then is carried away by the bait of the enticement. Then soon after, one will take the bait, give in to the temptation, and satisfy the lust of his flesh. It is for this reason that James writes then the desire when it has conceived gives birth to sin. James continues with the progression stating sin when it is fully-grown brings forth death. Once the desire is conceived, or once the individual gives acts upon that temptation by giving into its evil desire, it gives birth to sin that can lead to death.

James is telling these believers that once sin is conceived and begins to take root in the heart if it is not dealt with, it will become full grown within the heart, to attain what their hearts desire. James makes it very clear that once we give in to the temptation of that lust, it will inevitably give birth to sin. What was meant to produce pleasure and satisfaction, now only causes chaos and devastation. James warns these believers that the only result of fulfilling their lust brought about death. This death could for some have led to physical death depending upon the lust they were giving into. James has a deeper meaning in the fact that it was causing spiritual death to these believers when they gave into sin.

Again, we can see from Adam and Eve that when they ate of the fruit, they did so out of their desire and pleasure for power and control that stemmed from their lust. When they ate of the fruit, the promise of fulfillment only resulted in death. When Adam and Eve ate of the fruit, they faced spiritual death, in the fact that their sin had separated them from God. In turn, because of the curse, they would also suffer physical death due to their sin. James is warning these believers of the serious danger of temptation and the consequences if they were to give in to their lust. James wants his readers to understand that for the one who persisted in his temptation and living in that manner, and then, in the end, he would face eternal destruction. Paul wrote in Romans 7:20-21, "For when you were slaves of sin, you were free in regard to righteousness. Therefore, what benefit were you then deriving from the things of which you are now ashamed? For the outcome of those things is death."[116]

When we view pornography, let alone take up the time to get addicted, we are out for self-gratification, and we are, in no way, reflecting the Christian quality of love. The apostle Paul wrote,

1 Thessalonians 4:3-7 Updated American Standard Version (UASV)

[3] For this is the will of God, your sanctification; that is, that you abstain from sexual immorality;[117] [4] that each of you know how to possess his own vessel[118] in sanctification and honor, [5] not in lustful passion, just as also the Gentiles who do not know God; [6] that no man transgress and wrong his brother in the matter because the Lord is an avenger in all these things, just as we also told you before and solemnly warned you. [7] For God has not called us for impurity, but in sanctification.

Pornography especially takes selfish or unfair advantage of women and children, who are likely in abusive situations, for the personal gain of self-gratification. Simply objectifying them for your gratification is demeaning them. If you are using their images, you are also supporting whatever company exploits them, taking advantage of their circumstances. Just taking advantage of images, makes you indifferent, at worst a hater of women and a sexual deviant, toward the very people group that the Mosaic Law and Jesus Christ tried to protect.

Breaking the Habit

Some early Christians, prior to finding Christ, were 'unrighteous, sexually immoral, adulterers, men who practice homosexuality, and drunkards' However, they "were washed, you were sanctified, you were

---

[116] Thomas D. Lea, *THE BOOK OF JAMES*, vol. 17, CPH New Testament Commentary (Cambridge, OH: Christian Publishing House, 2017), 28-29.

[117] Gr *porneia, fornication*

[118] I.e. body

justified in the name of the Lord Jesus Christ and by the Spirit of our God."—1 Corinthians 6:9-11.

Psalm 55:22 Updated American Standard Version (UASV)

²² Cast your burden on Jehovah,
 and he will sustain you;
he will never permit
 the righteous to be shaken.

This begs the question, how do we throw our burdens on Jehovah, and how does he sustain us. How it is that he will not permit the righteous to be moved? In addition, if we are looking at porn, are we not unrighteous? Let us get ever closer to the answer.

1 Corinthians 10:13 Updated American Standard Version (UASV)

¹³ No temptation has overtaken you but such as is common to man; and God is faithful, who will not allow you to be tempted beyond what you are able, but with the temptation will provide the way of escape also, so that you will be able to endure it.

Many Christians, even very mature ones, as well as those leading congregations, have succumbed to pornography. Therefore, you should not feel alone in your battle to get control over your vessel.

Hebrews 4:12 Updated American Standard Version (UASV)

¹² For the word of God is living and active and sharper than any two-edged sword, and piercing as far as the division of soul and spirit, of both joints and marrow, and able to judge the thoughts and intentions of the heart.

This verse contains four statements about God's Word. First, it is **living.** God is a **living** God (Heb. 3:12). His message is dynamic and productive. It causes things to happen. It drives home warnings to the disobedient and promises to the believer. Second, God's Word is **active,** an emphasis virtually identical in meaning with the term **living.** God's Word is not something you passively hear and then ignore. It actively works in our lives, changes us, and sends us into action for God.

Third, God's Word penetrates the **soul and spirit.** To the Hebrew people, the body was a unity. We should not think of dividing the soul from the spirit. God's message is capable of penetrating the impenetrable. It can divide what is indivisible. Fourth, God's message is discerning. **It judges the thoughts and attitudes of the heart.** It passes judgment on our feelings and our thoughts. What we regard as secret

---

and hidden, God brought out for inspection by the discerning power of his Word.[119]

Requirements That Must Exist

Proverbs 2:1-2 Updated American Standard Version (UASV)

2 My son, if you receive my words
  and treasure up my commandments with you,
[2] making your ear attentive to wisdom
  and inclining your heart to discernment;[120]

After reading verses 1-5 of chapter 2, one can clearly see that it is their responsibility to acquire wisdom. *You* or *your* is found eleven times in these first five verses. Each of us is obligated to incline our ear, apply our heart, cry out for, lift our voice, seek, search for wisdom, and then we will understand the fear of Jehovah, the beginning of wisdom, and the knowledge of God we will find. All of this is found in God's Word. What exactly is wisdom though? It is the ability to make sensible decisions and judgments based on knowledge and experience, wisdom is sensibly applied knowledge. The genre of wisdom literature is found all throughout the Bible, but especially in the book of Job, Psalms, Proverbs, Ecclesiastes, and Song of Solomon. However, Wisdom is found in all of the genres of Scripture, even the life lessons within the narrative accounts.

In Chapter 1, Solomon gave his listeners a visual word picture of the consequences for those who do not listen to the corrective words of wisdom, warnings. Here in Chapter 2, he praises the incredible blessings and happiness that wisdom brings. In 2:1-4, Solomon lists three conditional clauses (requirements) that must exist or be brought about before it is possible that one can understand the fear of Jehovah and find the knowledge of God, each beginning with the word "if you (singular)" (vss 1, 3, 4). That is a big "if" because most of mankind pay no attention to God's Word. Clearly, it is up to you to seek wisdom and its handmaidens: discernment and understanding. First, "if you" are going to find joy in studying God's Word, you must be willing to receive Jehovah's words (the Bible) and treat it like it is a treasure that you would never wish to lose, valuing it above all else. **My words** refer to the Law (thoughts and ideas) that Solomon has embraced in an active faith and obedience, which he is teaching as well.

Are you really "attentive" and listening carefully when the Word of God is being explained at your Christian meetings? (Eph. 4:20-21) Do you

---

[119] Thomas A. Lea, vol. 10, *Hebrews & James*, Holman New Testament Commentary, 72 (Nashville: Broadman & Holman Publishers, 1999).

[120] The Hebrew word rendered here as "discernment" (*tevunah*) is related to the word *binah*, translated "understanding." Both appear in Proverbs 2:3.

'incline your heart [seat or center of intellect] to discernment' (commit yourself to), which is the insight, good sense, or wisdom to apply God's Word correctly. Of course, in order to incline your heart to discernment, you must be present at Christian meetings. (Proverbs 18:1) Thus, every Christian meeting can be a blessing for you if you are attentive and follow along in your Bibles. (Ac 2:1-4; Heb. 10:24-25. Being attentive means that you are paying attention, taking notice of (maybe taking notes in a tablet), and accepting the information as true and responding to it.

Having Insight, Good Sense, or Wisdom to Apply God's Word Correctly

Proverbs 2:3 Updated American Standard Version (UASV)

³ For if you cry for discernment[121]
    and raise your voice for understanding,

The second requirement or condition that must exist if we are to understand the fear of Jehovah and find the knowledge of God is to "cry for discernment," which, again is the insight, good sense, or wisdom to apply God's Word correctly. The Hebrew verb here (*qā·rā(ʾ)*) has the sense of loud, insistent crying or shouting that one needs help, begging that he be delivered from distress. Wisdom will be ours when our desire gets to the point where we are willing to cry aloud for it. The desperate one 'cries for discernment' to the truth of God's Word and applies it in his life. If we cannot recognize the importance and significance, the fullness of wisdom will elude us. **Discernment** (*bî·nā(h)*) is having the good sense or wisdom to respond properly to the Word of God. **Understanding** (*tᵉḇû·nā(h)*) is having the capacity for discerning a right course of action as the Word of God is applied appropriately. **Discernment** and **understanding** involve comprehending, perceiving, grasping what the authors meant, identifying individual verses in light of the whole, weighing or evaluating one verse in the light of the others.

Seeking and Searching

Proverbs 2:4 Updated American Standard Version (UASV)

⁴ if you keep seeking her like silver
    and searching for her as for hidden treasures,

The third requirement or condition that must exist if we are to understand the fear of Jehovah and find the knowledge of God is **seeking and searching for hidden treasure,** i.e., be committed and determined in one's quest. History has shown the lengths humans will go to in their quest to discover gold or silver. This makes us think of the mining exploits of men, such as those of the gold rushes in the early United States of American

---

[121] See 2.2 ftn.

history. Men have spent a lifetime trying to discover gold and silver. What actual value, though, does gold really have? Certainly, we can all agree that the knowledge of God demands far greater dedication and the treasure of eternal life is a far greater find. The knowledge of God is certainly a spiritual treasure. Therefore, we should have far more zeal as we seek wisdom, discernment, and understanding of God and his will. Solomon likens this knowledge to "hid treasures." The knowledge of God (hidden treasure) will not jump out of its place of hiding and deposit itself into the minds of those who are idle in their quest or search, it requires effort and perseverance on the part of those seeking and searching.

The "her" of **seeking her** and **searching for her** is a reference back to wisdom from verse 2. The imperfect Hebrew verb behind the English **seeking** (*bā·qǎš*) has the sense of diligently acquiring information, trying to get to or reach something that someone greatly desires. This verb is used when one is seeking information from God. (Ex. 33:7) in a similar but figurative sense, one may "seek" the face of God. (2 Sam. 21:1) Here (*bā·qǎš*) is used in reference to our searching for information, that is, a mental pursuit. The imperfect Hebrew verb behind the English **searching** (*hā·p̄ǎś*) has the sense of searching for, examining, trying to locate or discover information, in this case about the wisdom of God. The Hebrew noun behind the English **treasures** (*mǎṭ·môn*) has the sense of something of value that is hidden.

Searching for treasures requires discipline and determination. It calls for much digging be it actual treasure or seeking and searching for the knowledge of God, for "discernment," and for "understanding." This also demands much digging or getting below the surface knowledge. It is not sufficient to skim over the surface of God's Word. The invaluable treasures of the knowledge of God are for all who, like a determined, tenacious, resolute treasure hunter, are willing to seek them. Are we persistent in finding the knowledge of God? How can we improve our ability in doing so? Certainly, accurate knowledge of God and his Word is like a hidden treasure. What could be more valuable than the knowledge of God and Christ, which leads to eternal life? (John 17:3) Again, this treasure must also be sought for and discovered. Then, it must also be retained. It can also be expanded or grown. All of this means much effort on our part.

Carrying Out the "If You" Conditions

Proverbs 2:5 Updated American Standard Version (UASV)

[5] then you will understand the fear of Jehovah
and find the knowledge of God.

If you fulfill these three "if you" requirements or conditions of verses 1, 3, 4 and keep searching for, examining, trying to locate or discover information for wisdom, God says that you will finally understand the fear of Jehovah but will also find the knowledge of God. You are promised that you will gain God (2:5-8), and you will attain the wisdom of God. (2:9-11) The person searching for wisdom will find far more than mere human wisdom, as God is the source of all wisdom. When you enter the path that takes you deeper and deeper into the wisdom of God, you will find the very knowledge of God at the end of the path. When we recognize and accept the sovereignty of God, the fear of Jehovah, you will be ready to truly listen and accept him. Solomon identifies this treasure for you as "the knowledge of God," specifically, the truth about God and his will and purposes as revealed in the Bible. (2:5) There are numerous aspects to this treasure: true teachings, wise counsel, insight into the nature of God and his personality, as well as what lies ahead, and much more.

God Gives Wisdom to His Holy Ones

Proverbs 2:6-8 Updated American Standard Version (UASV)

⁶ For Jehovah gives wisdom;
   from his mouth come knowledge and understanding;
⁷ he stores up sound wisdom for the upright;
   he is a shield to those who walk in integrity,
⁸ guarding the paths of justice
   and watching over the way of his holy ones.

Jehovah represents himself symbolically as having a **mouth** (Heb. *pě(h)*) to convey to the reader about his communication, speech that gives you information, exhortation, counsel, or commands, which are contained in Scripture, wherein God speaks to you. (cf. Heb. 1:1-2; 2 Pet. 1:20-21) The **upright** (Heb. *yā·šār*) are God's true believers, his holy ones, who are diligently seeking and searching to know, love, and obey God and to live righteously as one can within their human imperfection. (Gen. 6:5; 8:21; Jer. 17:9; Rom. 5:12) You, the **holy one** is keeping the new covenant (Jer. 31.31; Heb. 8:8-12); thus, you know **wisdom**, which has served as a **shield** (Heb. *mā·ḡēn*) of defense from the offensive weapons of Satan, the world, and your own human imperfection, as you **walk** (Heb. *hā·lăk*) **in integrity** (Heb. *tōm*) a state of blamelessness being free of guilt, **guarding** (Heb. *nā·ṣăr*) you, making you safe from danger within your relationship with Jehovah (Ps 40:12) on the **paths of justice, watching** (Heb. *šā·măr*) over them. Hebrew terms relating to integrity have the root meaning of that which is "whole" or "complete." They often suggest moral soundness and uprightness. Those walking in **integrity** are unbending in devotion to Jehovah. For such blameless ones, he is a protective shield because they display true wisdom and conform to his righteous standards. This does not mean, though, that Jehovah will not allow you to be tested. He did so even with Job. "God is faithful," the apostle Paul noted to the Corinthians. In full he said, "No temptation has overtaken you but such as is common to man; and God is faithful, who will not allow you to be tempted beyond what you are able, but with the temptation will provide the way of escape also, so that you will be able to endure it." – 1 Corinthians 10:13.

Jehovah God will give wisdom to those, who are seeking and searching as though it were a hidden treasure. Imagine a gold mine in the side of a hill. If someone wanted enough money to have a meal or two, without working too hard, he could just pick up some specs of gold on the hillside. However, if he wanted a lifetime of meals, a life of financial security, he would be working in the mine daylight to dark. Sadly, when those searching for treasure crossed America to California in 1849, in search of gold, they soon discovered that the odds of striking it rich were ten thousand to one. It is quite different with Jehovah God, as he gives wisdom to all, "from his mouth come knowledge and understanding." Yes, God gives out wisdom free; he is the mine, for those that want to be wise.

We need to make this a part of our prayer life. The psalmist prayed, "Teach me your way, O Jehovah, that I may walk in your truth; unite my heart to fear your name." (Psalm 86:11) This is one prayer that we know will be answered. However, the answer will be based on the level that we act in harmony with our prayers. Are we willing to buy out the time to acquire wisdom, understanding, and discernment? A mere 30-60 minutes a day of Bible study will bring results that one might not have ever imagined. Are we willing to work 30 years to pay off a house, 40-45 years to receive a social security check (USA), but not 30-60 minutes a day, to acquire the wisdom of God that leads to eternal life?

Understanding What is Ethically and Morally Right and What is Wrong

Proverbs 2:9 Updated American Standard Version (UASV)

⁹ Then you will understand righteousness and justice
and equity, every good course;

This is true. After you have been studying the Bible for a while you begin to connect new information to things you already know. The truth of the Bible is so rational, reasonable, sensible, so interrelated, that the parts begin to fit together very quickly, and the entire purpose of God begins to become clear. As you maintain your studies, it becomes easier for you to make the right decisions that bring more happiness now. Also, your newfound wisdom will direct you away from useless, wrong life choices.

The first result from your search for wisdom is that of your finding the knowledge of God and the wisdom that he gives. (2:5-8) The second result in your quest for wisdom is that the very knowledge of God will enable you to discern, understand what is *ethically* (rules and principles in God's Word) and *morally* (moral compass that God gave you that you still possess a measure of in human imperfection) right and what is wrong. Your ability to judge what is right and wrong and act accordingly. This strong personal ethics of right and wrong in your dealings with others is described by righteousness and justice and equity. **Righteousness** (Heb. ṣĕ·ḏĕq) is when you adhere to the moral standard set out in God's Word. **Justice** (Heb. miš·pāṭ) is when you are free from partiality, selfishness, bias, as well as deception, where you make decisions that reflect God's sense of what is just. It is a case of fairness in your dealings with others. **Equity** (Heb. mê·šā·rîm) is a sense of fairness, being straight and upright, wherein you can make decisions that are **not** governed by discrimination or dishonesty. You do nothing that is sneaky, devious, deceitful, dishonest, morally uncertain.

How does God sustain us?

God sustains us by the Word of God, which contains the very knowledge of God, as explained in Hebrews 4:12 above. Thus, we need to discover the Bible verses that are applicable, and we then need to know what the author meant by the words that he used, as should have been understood by his original readers. In other words, we need to discover the original meaning. Then, we need to find the pattern of meaning that would apply to us. This is called working in behalf of our prayers. However, we are not done yet. We must be obedient to the Word of God. If we obey 50 percent, we will get 50 percent results. If we apply it 100 percent into our lives, we will get 100 percent results.

1 John 5:2 Updated American Standard Version (UASV)

² By this we know that we love the children of God, when we love God and do his commandments.

2 John 1:6 English Standard Version (ESV)

⁶ And this is love, that we walk according to his commandments. This is the commandment, just as you have heard from the beginning, that you should walk in it.

"What is love? It plays itself out in the real world in obedience. The essence of love is that we keep God's commandments. This glorifies God, is best for others, and is best for us. Everything God asks of us is intended to give something good to us or keep us from harm. First John presented the same emphasis on love and the same link between love and obedience." (Walls and Anders 1996, 237)

How it is that he will not permit the righteous to be moved?

God said he would never 'permit the righteous to be moved.' What is meant by 'move'?" It means to stumble or fall down spiritually or get into a practice of sin that you seem to be in. In other words, God will help you to become stable, steadfast, or unmovable, not giving into sin.

If we are looking at porn, are we not unrighteous?

No, this is not the case. We are all sinners, and God hates sin. However, he hates the **unrepentant** practice of sin. The unrighteous person is the one who lives in sin unrepentantly. If you are reading this, and you have been praying, trying to find a way to get control over yourself; then, you are not unrepentant. God makes allowance for our inherited sin from Adam, which means he understands our human weaknesses.

Thus, the steps are (1) Go to god fervently in prayer, (2) act in harmony with that prayer, by (3) research what the Bible offers toward recovery, (4) apply what you learn, and (5) get your stride again if you stumble, or get up when you fall down.

How often do you come across pornography?

- Never
- Sometimes,
- Rarely
- Daily,
- Weekly

Where do you come across pornography?

- Television,
- Stores,
- Internet,
- Cell phone,
- Email,
- Work,
- School,
- Other

Do you see a pattern of how these encounters come about, and how you deal with them?

Is there a pattern to your encounters?

146

Do you find yourself depressed or angry, so you look at pornography, because of the feeling that override the depression, even though you know, even worse depression is on the horizon for failing to be faithful. Do you receive email attachments from friends that contain pornography?

The good thing about the internet is that its filters are far better than ten years ago, In order to get a popup, or end up with wrong pages; you need to be very specific in your search. For example, if you Google "race cars," there will be links and images the movement that you get a few letters in. However, if you Google the word "porn," it will do nothing until you hit enter. The same is true with email, like Yahoo and Gmail. The ads in the margins are only reflective of sites that you have been visiting.

How do you react the moment that your eyes see pornography?

- You turn away immediately so that you could barely describe what you saw
- You look at it for a moment before turning away, and could better explain what you saw
- You continue to look until your desires lead you to search for more

The foremost thing that will help you to overcome the habit of viewing pornography is to appreciate the seriousness of it, as well as what your actions mean to you, to God, to your spouse, to your family, and to the victims in the images. You have to get to the point where you "hate evil."—Psalm 97:10.

Remove yourself from whatever results in the viewing of pornography.

Proverbs 22:3 English Standard Version (ESV)

³ The prudent sees danger and hides himself,
but the simple go on and suffer for it.

Be determined that you will not let your eyes fall upon pornography, and if they do unintentionally, you will immediately turn away.

Job 31:1 Good News Translation (GNT)

¹ I have made a solemn promise
never to look with lust at a woman.

Depending on your circumstances, you can apply the following as best you can.

- You only get on the internet when another is in the room
- You will place the computer in a public space
- You will leave your office door open
- You will immediate close out or delete anything inappropriate

- You will find a sponsor that can talk with you when you are feeling weak, stressed, or have stumbled

CHAPTER 20 The Self-Abuse of Masturbation

Masturbation is the sexual stimulation of one's own genitals, usually to the point of orgasm.

Is masturbation serious? Some Bible scholars view masturbation, saying, "the Hebrew and Christian Bibles are silent, neither denouncing nor encouraging the practice. The biblical story of Onan is traditionally linked to referring to masturbation and condemnation thereof, but the act described by this story is coitus interruptus, not masturbation."[122] Protestant "Theologians toward the middle of the 20th century began revising previous teachings, and some today even take pro-masturbation viewpoints. Some view it as an act of self-indulgence and even a sin of the flesh and believe that the practice is principally considered a sin because of its invitation to lust.[123] Those who view it within the range of allowable sexual behavior encourage it as a guard against adultery, pre-marital sex, or other forms of non-allowable sexual behavior, and as a method of balancing differing libidos between spouses."[124]

Before delving into the problems of masturbation, it is best that we consider some things first. It was God, who gave men and women, the natural desires of sexual attraction, as well as the physical pleasures, which are a result of stimulating certain parts of the body. However, Adam and Eve naturally leaned toward good, and would, therefore, have perfect control over their sexual desires. In fact, they did not even have clothes and went around naked. The first couple was together for a very long time in the Garden of Eden, before they sinned, and were expelled. It would seem that they never had relations throughout that time, as they would have likely procreated, and had children in the Garden of Eden. [125] Their desire for sexual attraction would not have been dysfunctional as that of imperfect humans after the fall, when sin entered the world. They were busy carrying out the duties that God had given them, like naming the animals, caring for the garden, knowing there was an eternity for the procreation, but knowing that they would sin one day. – Romans 5:12.

---

[122] Coogan, Michael (October 2010). God and Sex. What the Bible Really Says (1st ed.). New York, Boston: Twelve. Hachette Book Group. p. 110.
Ellens, J. Harold (2006). "6. Making Babies: Purposes of Sex". Sex in the Bible: a new consideration. Westport, Conn.: Praeger Publishers. p. 48.

[123] Miller, Jeff (2008). "Masturbation". Bible.org.

[124] Wright, Anne (2009). Grandma's Sex Handbook. Intimate Press. pp. 123–146.

[125] For a discussion on the length of the creation days, please see, http://bible-translation.net/page/part-2-genesis-1-1-is-the-earth-only-6-000-to-10-000-years-old-are-the-creative-days-literally-only-24-hours-long

Because Adam and Eve rebelled against the sovereignty of God, sin entered into the world, this means sexual desires were just the opposite of their descendants, for we have inherited the disease of sin, missing the mark of perfection. (Gen. 6:5, AT) "When the Lord saw that the wickedness of man on the earth was great and that **the whole bent of his thinking was never anything but evil . . . ."** (Gen. 8:21, AT) ". . . **the bent of man's mind may be evil from his very youth. . . ."** (Jer. 17:9, ESV) The **heart is deceitful** above all things, and it is exceedingly corrupt: who can know it?

The main reason for sexual intercourse between a man and a woman is to procreate and fill the earth. Being that God is the Creator of all, including humans, he has the right to set the moral standards of what is good and what is bad. Of Course, Adam and Eve disregarded this, when their rebellion demonstrated that they felt that they did not need his standards but could determine for themselves what is good and what is bad. The Bible is quite clear that sexual relations are to be between one man and one woman, who are married. Anything outside of that would be adultery if married, or fornication if unmarried.

The imperfect human lacks the self-control that perfect Adam and Eve displayed. Those who are single have sexual desires that are not able to be satisfied. In fact, the male human body has a way of dealing with such stress to the body, which is by nocturnal emission of semen. Is masturbation another way for single men and women, to deal with the stress and frustration of pent up sexual desires? No. While it is true, that masturbation does no physical harm if practiced in moderation. However, as Christians, we are not concerned with the physical aspect, but rather the spiritual aspect.

The Bible on Masturbation

The Bible condemns quite clearly such sexual sins as fornication, adultery, homosexuality, and bestiality, masturbation is not mentioned. (Genesis 39:7-9; Leviticus 18:20, 22-23; 1 Corinthians 6:9-10) Another factor to consider is that the language of the New Testament, Koine Greek, contained several words to describe the practice masturbation in the Greek-speaking world, but they are not used in the New Testament.

While the opinion of most physicians is that masturbation is harmless physically, it seems that the human conscience rejects it, as most are not as comfortable talking about masturbation as they are about another bodily function, like washing your hands. If you doubt me, the next time you are at a restaurant, and the women excuse themselves to freshen up, when they return, ask them if they masturbated. If it is as natural, you will not have any reservations about asking, and they will not have any embarrassed or angry looks on their face. This may sound extreme, but it makes the point.

150

Adam and Eve were created in the image of God and were a reflection of his qualities and attributes. Even after the fall, in our state of imperfection, all humans still maintain a good measure of that image. We all have a moral nature, which produces the faculty of conscience. This moral nature and associated conscience are seen in that most countries have laws that are based on the Bible's moral values, do not kill, do not steal, and do not commit adultery, and so on. Why is it that most people feel guilty, ashamed, dirty, embarrassed, or abnormal when discussing masturbation? It is the conscience that God gave us.

Put to Death Evil Desire

Colossians 3:5 Updated American Standard Version (UASV)

⁵ Deaden, therefore, your members on the earth: sexual immorality [Gr *porneia*], uncleanness, passion, evil desire, and greediness, which is idolatry.

> The ... two words belong together. "Lust" (*epithymia*) and "passions" (*pathos*) or "evil desires," as translated in the NIV, generally refer to strong desires gone bad. Although the word can, on occasion, be used of an honorable desire (1 Tim 3:1), the normal use is negative. It refers most often to the misdirected fulfillment of bodily appetites, usually sexual appetites. A passion is uncontrolled and habitual lust. When lust goes unchecked, a passion for what is forbidden arises. Habits are formed which feed each other. Lust encourages passion, and passion produces more perverted lust.[126]

"Deaden, therefore, your body members," urges the Bible, "as respects . . . **sexual appetite**." (Colossians 3:5) This "sexual appetite" is not the new sexual sensations that most youths feel during puberty, of which there is no need to be ashamed. "Sexual appetite" exists when these feelings are intensified so that one loses control. Such sexual appetite has led to gross sexual immorality, as described by Paul at Romans 1:26, 27.

However, does not masturbation "put to death" these "evil desires"? Hardly, in order to masturbate, one must feed his mind on evil desires, as well as pornographic images. Like any addiction, it takes stronger content to achieve the same gratification. If you drink one beer a day, soon you will have to move on to two, to get the same feeling. If you look at pornographic images, soon they will have to be viler, to achieve the same results. Eventually, you will need the real thing because the imagination is

---

126 Richard R. Melick, Jr, vol. 32, Philippians, Colossians, Philemon, The New American Commentary, 291 (Nashville: Broadman & Holman Publishers, 1993).

not achieving the same outcome. The world is full of opportunity, where you will find yourself aroused in a wrong moment or an inconvenient time, and you will commit fornication if single, or adultery if married.

Your Thoughts Will Lead You Astray

Moreover, your using women objectively in your imagination will carry over into the real world. Masturbation means that you need to view and think of women as a tool, as a means to an end, as opposed to sensitive human beings. In addition, you will start to see your own body as an object as well, a means to self-gratification. Self-abuse is self-centered. The person loses sight of love and moves toward sexual pleasures. Our Creator intended man and woman to find their sexual satisfactions within the marriage bed, and within expressions of love.

How does God view our human weaknesses?

Psalm 86:5 Updated American Standard Version (UASV)

[5] For you, O Jehovah, are good, and ready to forgive,
and abundant in lovingkindness to all who call upon you.

When we slip up and fall short, succumbing to masturbation, we certainly feel guilty, which is appropriate. However, we do not want to beat ourselves down to where anxiety and stress cause future failures.

1 John 3:20 Updated American Standard Version (UASV)

[20] in whatever our heart condemns us; for God is greater than our heart and knows all things.

We may find ourselves falling short on masturbation many times, as it has a stronger hold on us than we may have realized. This results in our feeling guilty, ashamed, dirty, embarrassed, or abnormal. We do not feel worthy of God's Love. We need not think that God is no longer forgiving us, as this is exactly what Satan would like. The fact that you feel as distraught as you do means that God still loves you, and you have not committed the unforgivable sin. Simply be steadfast in the process of overcoming this habit, and continue fervently to go to God in prayer, begging him for forgiveness and cleansing and help. However, we as imperfect humans can be accredited a righteous standing before God, being accepted back into the family of God. **He makes allowances** for our imperfection.

Below is how he views a repentant sinner,

Psalm 103:9-12 Updated American Standard Version (UASV)

[9] He will not always find fault,
nor will he keep his anger forever.

¹⁰ He does not deal with us according to our sins,
    nor repaid us according to our errors.[127]
¹¹ For as high as the heavens are above the earth,
    So great is his lovingkindness toward those who fear him.
¹² As far as the east is from the west,
    so far does he remove our transgressions from us.

      Isaiah 38:17 Updated American Standard Version (UASV)

¹⁷ Look, it was for my welfare
    that I had great bitterness;
but in love you have delivered my soul
    from the pit of destruction,
for you have cast all my sins
    behind your back.

      Micah 7:18-19 Updated American Standard Version (UASV)

¹⁸ Who is a God like you, pardoning error
    and passing over transgression[128]
    for the remnant of his inheritance?
He does not retain his anger forever,
    because he delights in lovingkindness.
¹⁹ He will again have compassion on us;
    he will tread our iniquities underfoot.
You will cast all our sins
    into the depths of the sea.

    You will notice in Psalm 103:12, that God removes the sins of the repentant one as far as the east is from the west. The picture being painted is, to the human mind that is the farthest you can remove something as there is no greater distance. In Isaiah 38, we are given another visual, God throwing our sins behind his back, meaning he can no longer see them, as

---

[127] **Error:** (Heb., *ʼāwōn;* Gr. *anomia, paranomia*) The Hebrew word *awon* essentially relates to erring, acting illegally or wrongly. This aspect of sin refers to committing a perverseness, wrongness, lawlessness, law breaking, which can also include the rejection of the sovereignty of God. It also focuses on the liability or guilt of one's wicked, wrongful act. This error may be deliberate or accidental; either willful deviation of what is right or unknowingly making a mistake. (Lev. 4:13-35; 5:1-6, 14-19; Num. 15:22-29; Ps 19:12, 13) Of course, if it is intentional; then, the consequence is far more serious. (Num. 15:30-31) Error is in opposition to the truth, and those willfully sinning corrupt the truth, a course that only brings forth flagrant sin. (Isa 5:18-23) We can be hardened by the deceitfulness of sin.–Ex 9:27, 34-35; Heb. 3:13-15.

[128] **Transgression:** (Heb. *ʼavar,* Gr. *parabasis*) Sin can take the form of a "transgression." This is an overstepping, namely, to exceed a moral limit or boundary. Biblically speaking, this would be crossing the line and saying, feeling, thinking or doing something that is contrary to God's personality, standards, ways, will and purposes, as set out in the Scriptures. It is breaking God's moral law.–Num. 14:41; Deut. 17:2, 3; Josh. 7:11, 15; 1 Sam 15:24; Isa 24:5; Jer. 34:18; Rom. 2:23; 4:15; 5:14; Gal. 3:19; 1 Tim. 2:14; Heb. 2:2; 9:15.

they are out of sight, thus out of mind. In Micah, our last example, we see that God hurls all of the sins of a repentant person into the depths of the sea. In the setting of the ancient person, this meant that retrieving them was literally impossible. In other words, God has removed them, never to be retrieved or brought to mind ever again. This was the viewpoint that he had before Jesus ever even offered himself as a ransom sacrifice.

However, just because God is so forgiving, this will never justify sinning unrepentantly, as his patience will wear our, or the evil age of Satan will end when we least expect it. He hopes that you will continue to work toward setting aside the habit of masturbation, as it is an unclean habit.

Bibliography

Anders, M. (1999). *Holman New Testament Commentary: vol. 8, Galatians, Ephesians, Philippians, Colossians.* Nashville, TN: Broadman & Holman Publishers.

Anders, M. (2005). *Holman Old Testament Commentary - Proverbs .* Nashville: B&H Publishing.

Anders, M., & Butler, T. (2002). *Holman Old Testament Commentary: Isaiah.* Nashiville, TN: B&H Publishing.

Anders, M., & Lawson, S. (2004). *Holman Old Testament Commentary - Psalms: 11.* Grand Rapids: B&H Publishing.

Anders, M., & McIntosh, D. (2009). *Holman Old Testament Commentary - Deuteronomy.* Nashville: B&H Publishing.

Andrews, S. J., & Bergen, R. D. (2009). *Holman Old Testament Commentary: 1-2 Samuel.* Nashville: Broadman & Holman.

Boa, K., & Kruidenier, W. (2000). *Holman New Testament Commentary: Romans.* Nashville: Broadman & Holman.

Brand, C., Draper, C., & Archie, E. (2003). *Holman Illustrated Bible Dictionary: Revised, Updated and Expanded.* Nashville, TN: Holman.

Butler, T. C. (2000). *Holman New Testament Commentary: Luke.* Nashville, TN: Broadman & Holman Publishers.

Butler, T. C. (2005). *Holman Old Testament Commentary - Hosea, Joel, Amos, Obadiah, Jonah, Micah .* Nashville: Broadman & Holman Publishers.

Clinton, T., & Ohlschlager, G. (2008). *Competent Christian Counseling; Volume One: Foundations and Practice of Compassionate Soul Care.* Colorado Springs, CO: WaterBrook Press.

Cooper, R. (2000). *Holman New Testament Commentary: Mark.* Nashville: Broadman & Holman Publishers.

Easley, K. H. (1998). *Holman New Testament Commentary, vol. 12, Revelation.* (Nashville, TN: Broadman & Holman Publishers.

Gangel, K. O. (1998). *Holman New Testament Commentary: Acts.* Nashville, TN: Broadman & Holman Publishers.

Gangel, K. O. (2000). *Holman New Testament Commentary, vol. 4, John* . Nashville, TN: Broadman & Holman Publishers.

Garland, D. E. (2003). *1 Corinthians, Baker Exegetical Commentary on the New Testament.* Grand Rapids, MI: : Baker Academic.

Garland, D. E., & Longman, T. I. (2008). *The Expositor's Bible Commentary: Proverbs-Isaiah.* Grand Rapids, MI: Zondervan.

Harley, W. F. (2011). *His Needs, Her Needs: Building an Affair-Proof Marriage.* Grand Rapids, MI: Revell.

Larson, K. (2000). *Holman New Testament Commentary, vol. 9, I & II Thessalonians, I & II Timothy, Titus, Philemon.* Nashville, TN: Broadman & Holman Publishers.

Lea, T. D. (1999). *Holman New Testament Commentary: Vol. 10, Hebrews, James.* Nashville, TN: Broadman & Holman Publishers.

Martin, G. S. (2002). *Holman Old Testament Commentary: Numbers.* Nashville: Broadman & Holman Publishers.

McMinn, M. R. (2010). *Psychology, Theology, and Spirituality in Christian Counseling (AACC Library).* Carol Stream, IL: Tyndale House Publishers.

Pratt Jr, R. L. (2000). *Holman New Testament Commentary: I & II Corinthians, vol. 7.* Nashville: Broadman & Holman Publishers.

Walls, D., & Anders, M. (1996). *Holman New Testament Commentary: I & II Peter, I, II & III John, Jude.* Nashville: Broadman & Holman Publishers.

Weber, S. K. (2000). *Holman New Testament Commentary, vol. 1, Matthew.* Nashville, TN: Broadman & Holman Publishers.